Longman exam practice kits

A-Level Sociology

Stephen Harris

LONGMAN

Series Editors
Geoff Black and Stuart Wall

Titles available
A-level
Biology
Business Studies
Chemistry
Mathematics
Psychology
Sociology

Addison Wesley Longman Ltd.,
Edinburgh Gate, Harlow,
Essex CM20 2JE, England
and Associated Companies throughout the World.

© Addison Wesley Longman 1997

First Published 1997

ISBN 0582-30382-6

British Library Cataloguing-in-Publication Data
A catalogue record for this book is available from the British Library.

Set by 8 in 11/13pt Baskerville
Produced by Longman Asia Ltd, Hong Kong

Contents

How to use this book

This book seeks to help you achieve a good grade in your A-level Sociology examination. The book covers the major topics in A-level Sociology which are common to all the examination boards and some other topics most likely to be examined. The book is arranged in four parts.

Part I Preparing for the examination

Here I consider some useful techniques you might use before and during the examination. A Revision Planner is provided to help you structure your run-up to the exam. The different *types* of question you will face are considered, along with the techniques you will need to answer each type of question successfully. It is vital that you correctly interpret the questions that are set, so I define some of the key words you are likely to find in questions, such as *analyse* and *evaluate*.

Part II Topic areas, summaries and questions

Here, I identify eight key topic areas: theory and methods; the family; education; social stratification; poverty, welfare and social policy; power and politics; religion; and deviance, crime and social control. For *each* of these topic areas you will find the following:

1 **Revision tips,** giving specific guidance on revising that particular topic area;
2 **Topic outline,** briefly summarizing the key points of theory and practice in that topic area;
3 **Revision activity,** to help make your revision active, an exercise which will help you self-check your understanding of that topic area; and
4 **Practice questions,** from recent papers of the type you are likely to encounter in your exam.

It is essential that you try the questions yourself before checking with the answers provided to all activities and questions in Part III of the book.

Part III Answers and grading

Here you will find answers to the activities and practice questions set for each topic area. Some of these will be actual student answers with examiner comments, helping you to identify the strengths and weaknesses in the answer. Other answers will be outline answers from the examiners to indicate what they were looking for in the question.

You will also find comments from *mark schemes* or other guidance on how the examiners would seek to distinguish between answers at one grade as compared to some other grade.

Part IV Timed practice question papers with answers

Here you will find papers or parts of papers, which will give you practice in timing yourself under exam-type conditions *before* the exam. Outline answers and a breakdown of the marks awarded are provided to these questions so that you can check your performance.

part I

Preparing for the examination

Planning your revision

▶ Start revising in good time. Last-minute revision works for some people but, on the whole, it is too risky. In any case you need to develop the appropriate skills through practice.

▶ Try to allocate set times during the week when you revise your sociology. If you are doing other subjects, check you have enough revision slots to cover them all.

▶ Be clear about what you need to learn in terms of skills as well as topics. Prepare more than the bare minimum of topics required so you have some choice in your examinations and can avoid awkward questions.

▶ Plan your revision carefully and as early as possible. Use the Revision Planner in this book to organize your revision on a week-by-week basis.

▶ Review your plan regularly and adapt it as necessary. Some topics and activities will take more or less time than you predict. Your plan should be realistic and include opportunities for relaxation and fun. If your exam is in the summer, take advantage of the long, light evenings to get some fresh air and exercise.

▶ *Revise actively.* It is not a good idea merely to read through your notes and hope you absorb the knowledge. Now all the sociology syllabuses examine skills as well as knowledge, it is essential to practise these.

▶ Practise with the help of past questions. This book gives you the opportunity to do this. Whole papers and even whole questions may appear daunting at first, so you might try parts of structured or data-response questions. Make sure that the length of your answer reflects the marks allocated to that part of the question. As the exam approaches, try to use the appropriate time for your answer.

▶ Teachers try to reinforce learning by getting you to use more than one of your senses.

▶ You can make use of tapes (your own or commercially prepared ones) and discussion with friends.

▶ Summarize your notes in tables, charts and diagrams to help provide a visual image you can remember easily.

▶ If you have a sensory impairment, try to work out some equivalent activities with your teachers or communicators.

▶ Practise your sociological skills when you are 'off-duty'. Use sociological concepts to analyse everyday life, for example:
 – Consumerism – shopping
 – Culture – getting 'dressed-up'
 – Expressive relationships – on the dance floor or arguing with parents.

▶ Cut out useful examples from the media which can be applied to questions, for example, recent poverty figures, or events which can be used in the debates about the role of religion.

▶ Once you have covered the major points of a topic and feel confident, it may help to choose some difficult or unpredictable past questions or parts of structured questions to practise making the best of a difficult question.

Using examination questions in revision

After you have revised a topic area it is vital that you are able to apply your knowledge and understanding in a critical manner to a set question.

Try the typical questions you will find in Part II and then check your answers against the various suggestions in Part III. Practising with past questions makes your revision active and has a number of advantages.

▶ It provides a check on your understanding as well as your knowledge.

▶ It may reveal gaps in your knowledge and weaknesses in one or more of the skills. Use this feedback to review your revision plan.

▶ You may be clearer about the number of topics you need to revise to allow you to avoid difficult questions.

▶ You will become familiar with the style and language used in questions. The instruction words used in questions are listed and explained later in this section.

▶ Checking your answers with the suggestions and comments in Part III will give you an insight into what the examiners are looking for. You can see this in more detail in mark schemes and chief examiners' reports.

▶ As the examination approaches you can practise the experience by completing the timed examination papers in Part IV.

Types of examination questions

Essays

This is the traditional type of examination question and is used by all the examination boards.

▶ It is very important that you *focus your answer on the set question*. Every year chief examiners' reports comment that some candidates write out a prepared answer which does not address the set question. Sometimes these are just generalized accounts of knowledge on the topic. Sometimes the answer is to last year's question or the question the candidate would have liked to see!

▶ *Plan* your answer to ensure you can answer the question and that your response is:
  – **relevant**
  – **logical**
  – **coherent**
  – **balanced and**
  – **critical**.

▶ Quality of language is assessed in A-level Sociology. This includes spelling, punctuation and grammar. It is also necessary to express your ideas clearly and use a broad range of sociological conceptual terms in a precise way.

Structured questions

Here a question is broken down into a series of components which may test different parts of the topic and different skills. Usually the mark for the component is provided and this indicates the length of response expected.

Data-response questions

You are presented with a number of items which may be in a variety of forms: text, graphs or tables. Questions require detailed reference to the items, for example, the interpretation of statistics or the evaluation of ideas presented in the text. Again the question is broken down into a series of components which may test different parts of the topic and different skills.

Research design

This is required by the IBS for students who do not take the coursework option. It asks them to apply their knowledge and understanding of research methodology to a set task. As well as revising your theory and methods notes, you should practise past examples of designing research.

Coursework

This is assessed by the examiners or by your teacher and moderated by the examination board.

Assessment objectives and marking schemes

Assessment objectives and the methods used by examiners to mark them are now published for the benefit of students and teachers. Although they tend to be expressed in rather technical language it is worth being familiar with those abilities that examiners value and for which they award marks. You will find this information in syllabuses and mark schemes.

The various examinations tend to reward:

▶ knowledge and understanding of concepts, studies and theories;
▶ understanding of data;
▶ interpretation of data;
▶ application of concepts and theories to sociological and social problems;
▶ analysis of sociological issues and personal experience; and
▶ evaluation of theories, methods' evidence and arguments.

For example, the AEB awards marks as follows:

	Marks for data-response questions	Marks for essays
1 Knowledge and understanding	5	9
2 Interpretation and application	10	9
3 Evaluation	10	9
	Total 25	Up to total of 25

This should make it clear that you cannot do well just by learning prepared descriptions of studies and theories. You must answer the set question; this will enable you to gain marks for each of the three skills.

Knowledge and understanding

You should show that you know and understand sociological concepts, studies, methods, theories and the main arguments of sociological debates. You can demonstrate understanding by presenting evidence and arguments in a logical and coherent way. You do not need to know studies in minute detail. Particularly for the data-response questions you need a broad understanding of major issues.

Interpretation and application

These skills are concerned with how effectively you can use knowledge to answer a set question. Interpretation on data-response questions usually involves using data in the form of text, tables or graphs to answer a question. Calculations are rare and usually very simple. Interpretation and application on the essay paper might involve choosing an appropriate study (maybe from a different topic) and using it to answer the question.

You will often have the opportunity to apply sociological theories of your knowledge of methods to a specific topic area. You may also apply current affairs and personal experience as long as they are used to make a sociological point. Chapter 7 on religion shows how classical sociological theories can be examined in the light of recent events.

Evaluation

This is being critical. Evaluation may take the form of a specific critical point or a more general evaluative framework in an answer. Often you can use alternative theories or approaches to criticize a particular explanation. For example, use feminist approaches to criticize functionalist views on the family.

Criticism can be positive as well as negative. You should get into the habit of considering the strengths and weaknesses of methods, studies and theories.

Weak evaluation often takes the form of listing alternatives. This should be improved by linking arguments. Good evaluative words include: *however, whereas, on the other hand, this can be challenged by.*

The basis of criticism can be:

▶ **Empirical** – factual, based on evidence;
▶ **Methodological** – the way data was gathered and interpreted;
▶ **Theoretical** – challenging assumptions of, say, consensus or conflict approaches; and
▶ **Ideological** – where disagreement is based on values.

Incidentally, to gain maximum marks you need *not* achieve perfection or be as competent as the chief examiner. The AEB standard is based on the best that could be achieved by an 18-year-old student who has studied the subject for two years. Therefore, full marks *are* attainable for part or whole questions.

Command words used in sociology examinations

Argue	Use evidence and explanations to make a case.
Account for	Explain, rather than just describe, a sociological or social phenomenon. Answer the question 'why?'
Analyse	Show you understand a complicated issue by breaking it down into simple component parts. Identify and explain any relationships between the parts.
Assess	Examine the strengths and weaknesses of evidence or an argument. This is a common instruction to encourage you to evaluate rather than just describe.
Compare	Identify similarities.
Contrast	Identify differences, usually paired with 'compare'. Do not just juxtapose two alternatives but explicitly point out the similarities and differences.
Criticize	Offer arguments for and against. This term is often added to 'analyse', 'examine' or 'explain'.
Discuss	Present at least two views on an issue and look at their strengths and weaknesses.
Evaluate	You must make a judgement based on the quality of evidence and argument. More or less the same as 'assess'.
Examine	Take an in-depth view of, for example, the relationship between two variables.
Identify	State a point or an example.
Illustrate	Cite relevant sociological examples.
Outline	Provide a brief description of, for example, an explanation. Usually combined with an instruction to be critical.

During the examination

▶ Try to relax. Replacing last minute revision with a walk or a video may help to control tension. Some stress is natural and will help your performance.
▶ Read the rubric – the instructions at the beginning of the examination paper. This should be familiar to you from previous papers.

- ▶ Choose your questions. It may help to attempt a brief plan for an essay to ensure you can do it.
- ▶ Plan your time carefully. Jot down when you should start each question and keep to your schedule.
- ▶ Plan your first answer. It does not matter which order you attempt questions.
- ▶ Answer the set question. When planning and writing essays, refer back to the question at regular intervals to make sure you are focusing on the set question.
- ▶ Remember to demonstrate all your skills, not just your knowledge of studies and theories.

part II

Topic areas, summaries and questions

Theory and methods

REVISION TIPS

An understanding of sociological theory and the relationship between theory and research methods is an essential requirement for A- and A/S level Sociology. The AEB has a compulsory theory and methods question as well as coursework and examination options which are also focused on theory and methods issues. The IBS syllabus offers the choice between demonstrating knowledge of theory and methods in coursework or in Paper 3.

All the syllabuses are explicit in their requirement that knowledge and understanding of theoretical and methodological issues should be applied to questions on other substantive topics. This should not be seen as just another awkward obstacle to be overcome but the opportunity to use theoretical frameworks to organize answers in a logical and critical way.

You will find yourself practising the evaluation of theories when working on other topics, although you should not be tempted to try to include all theories to answer all questions. You still need to make informed judgements on which approaches to include and how much emphasis should be put on them.

There are no 'best' studies to use when illustrating the use of methods. You will find it useful to employ studies you have learned for other topics and/or used for your coursework.

Key words and their definitions

Structuralist perspectives   see the social world as existing independently of individuals whose behaviour is constrained by external social forces.

Action perspectives   see the construction of the social world as being the result of a process where individuals attribute meaning to the behaviour of themselves and others.

Consensus theories   see society as normally harmonious with social order based on shared values.

Conflict theories   see conflict as normal with social order being imposed by the more powerful on weaker members of society.

Positivist approaches   involve the use of methods similar to those used in the natural sciences to test hypotheses. Social facts are studied.

Interpretive approaches   involve the search for the subjective meanings which are attributed to behaviour. Social action is studied.

Value freedom   the idea that sociological research should not be influenced by the moral or political views of the researcher.

TOPIC OUTLINE

The major themes of questions are as follows:

Evaluation of sociological theoretical approaches including discussion of:

▶ structure and action;
▶ consensus and conflict; and
▶ positivism and interpretivism.

Assessment of the strengths and weaknesses of a range of sociological research methods including discussion of:

▶ primary and secondary research;
▶ quantitative and qualitative methods; and
▶ the relationship between theory and research methods.

A consideration of the nature of sociology including debates on:

▶ sociology as a science;
▶ value freedom; and
▶ sociology and social policy.

1 Theories

For each of the major theories you should be able to:

▶ identify the main assumptions;
▶ identify some major criticisms, both positive and negative;
▶ identify different interpretations or versions of the theory; and
▶ illustrate your answers with reference to sociological research from other topics you are revising.

A-level questions frequently require knowledge and understanding of:

Functionalism
Marxism
Interactionist theories
Feminism

You may be rewarded if you are able to refer to other theories which are currently less significant at A-level, such as:

New Right theories
Postmodernism

There have been examination questions that specify new right approaches, and Postmodernism is often mentioned in syllabuses and mark schemes.

2 Methods

Many questions require the candidate to evaluate a particular method or group of methods. In order to organize an answer to such a question, you might try the following framework:

	Advantages Strengths Uses	Disadvantages Weaknesses Limitations
Theoretical considerations		
Practical constraints		
Ethical issues		

An example of how you can begin to apply this framework to the method *participant observation* is given below.

Discussions about the relationships between theory and methods are dominated by the debate between *positivist* and *interpretive sociology*.

> *Positivist sociologists* prefer methods which can be employed scientifically. Research should be reliable, valid, generalizable and above all verifiable, e.g. Durkheim chose the comparative survey method using official statistics. This is also consistent with his functionalist perspective on society, as he sees the behaviour of individuals as being constrained by external structural influences.
>
> *Interpretive sociologists* choose methods which provide insights into the social construction of reality by revealing the subjective experience of those studied. They are looking for the ways in which actors attribute meaning to their own, and others' behaviour, and at the commonsense assumptions which underlie the way people define social situations, e.g. Becker chose participant observation to study deviants by sharing their experiences. Sacks chose to study conversation between potential suicides and staff at a suicide-prevention centre.

You need to be able to explain and illustrate:

▶ *positivists'* preference for *scientific* and *quantitative* research; and
▶ *interpretivists'* preference for *subjective* and *qualitative* research.

A more recent debate is about the preference of *feminists* for research methods which allow women to speak for themselves. This often involves a rejection of the scientific approach.

An assessment of the usefulness of participant observation

	Advantages Strengths Uses	Disadvantages Weaknesses Limitations
Theoretical considerations	1 Provides insight into meanings attributed to social action 2	1 Not scientific 2
Practical constraints	1 Can study natural behaviour 2	1 Problems of access 2
Ethical issues	1 Allows subjects to speak for themselves 2	1 Deceives subjects 2

I have only begun this exercise. You could complete the table for participant observation and try to do the same thing for other individual methods, such as interviews, or for groups of methods such as those which use secondary data.

3 The nature of sociology

Sociology and science
You should be able to outline and discuss the following issues:

▶ Can sociological research use the logic and procedures of the natural sciences?
▶ What are the theoretical and practical problems that arise when sociologists employ scientific methodology?
▶ What is science?

Sociology and value freedom
The main issues here are:

▶ Should sociology be value free?
▶ Is sociology inevitably ideological?
▶ What are the causes of bias in sociological research?
▶ What are the effects of bias in sociological research?

Sociology and social policy
The main issues here are:

▶ What is the difference between sociological problems and social problems?
▶ Should sociology try to change the world?
▶ How does sociology help to define social problems?
▶ How has sociology influenced social policy?

These three major areas should not be seen as separate. They are all related to each other as well as to other methodological and theoretical issues.

REVISION ACTIVITY

When sociologists choose one or more research methods their choice depends on a number of factors. There is no best method. Some sociologists wish to minimize *involvement* with their subjects, while others wish to maximize it.

The diagram is intended to suggest that there is a continuum of methods available depending on the extent to which they are seen as 'scientific'.

Arrange the following methods in order, according to how scientific they are. Place the number of the most scientific method in the left-hand box, and so on.

1 Structured interview with closed questions
2 Participant observation
3 Survey using official statistics
4 Unstructured interview
5 Postal questionnaire
6 Non-participant observation
7 Structured interview with open questions

More Scientific	**More Interpretive/Meaningful**
Quantitative	Qualitative
Detached	Involved
Objective	Subjective
Reliable	Understanding
Representative	In-depth

☐ ☐ ☐ ☐ ☐ ☐ ☐

EXAMINATION QUESTIONS

Question 1
'The purpose of the experiment is to create a standardized situation for the researcher to study, in which variables are under the control of the experimenter.' Evaluate the contribution experiments make to a sociological understanding of social behaviour. (IBS, 1996)

Question 2
Evaluate the ways in which scientific thinking and methods have influenced sociological research. (*25 marks*) (AEB, 1995)

Question 3
Answer *all* parts of this question.

Item A

It hardly needs emphasizing how much the success of the participant observer's approach depends on his or her skill and personality. If these command the respect and friendship of those being observed, and if they are combined with an ability to interpret and describe what is seen, the method enables the presentation of a picture of social reality at once more vivid,   5
complete and authentic than is possible with other methods. But any defects in his or her approach and ability can easily arouse suspicion, and so undermines the study. Participant observation is a highly individual technique.

Item B

Books and accounts that derive from participant observation studies are often profusely illustrated with extracts from the conversations of those being studied. The richness and immediacy of these materials serve to provide a window on the world that is being observed. By quoting in detail the words of 'witness', the reader is given access to the meanings and interpretations of the community being studied, or so it is hoped. In some cases the extracts will be organized according to certain theoretical considerations, as in Paul Willis's *Learning to Labour*. Other researchers present their arguments virtually entirely in the words of those in whom they are interested. Seabrook's study of a working-class childhood is a case in point. It could be maintained that this   10
material lets the data speak for itself; the reader can make his/her own judgements. However, these techniques of recording and presenting data are also subject to a number of criticisms.

Source: adapted from Murray Morison, *Methods in Sociology*, (Longman) 1989.

Item C

Quantitative methods are associated with research that can be expressed in statistical or numerical form, or can be 'measured' in some way, such as age, qualifications or income. The results of such methods are usually presented as data in the form of statistical tables, pie charts and bar charts. Sociologists who favour quantitative methods argue that they not only allow appropriate   5
'measurements' to be made, but that conclusions can also be drawn on the relationships between different social variables. For these and other reasons, these sociologists favour the social survey as the main method of quantitative research.

(a) Suggest *two* reasons why participant observation is 'a highly individual technique' *(Item A, line 8). (2 marks)*
(b) Identify *two* criticisms of letting 'the data speak for itself' in participant observation studies *(Item B, line 11). (2 marks)*
(c) Suggest *two* problems that might be experienced by a researcher in undertaking covert participant observation. *(2 marks)*
(d) With reference to *Item C* and elsewhere, assess the advantages and disadvantages of quantitative methods of social investigation. *(9 marks)*
(e) With reference to the Items and other sources, evaluate the claim that in participant-observation studies, what is gained in terms of validity is lost in reliability. *(10 marks)*

Total: 25 marks
(AEB, 1996)

2 The family

REVISION TIPS

Family questions often demand knowledge and understanding of:

► inequalities based on *gender*, with an emphasis on the position of girls and women;
► inequalities based on *age*, with an emphasis on children and the old;
► differences, rather than inequalities, based on *ethnicity*; and
► differences, rather than inequalities, based on *class*.

Many of the explanations and studies of the family are *ideological*. Assessment of ideologically opposed approaches can provide a good basis for evaluative answers.

The arguments between functionalism and Marxism are useful in analysing the functions of families.

The arguments between the new right and feminism are useful in examining issues such as single parent families.

Key words and their definitions

Family   a group of individuals related to one another by 'blood', marriage or adoption. Nuclear and extended families are different kinds of family structures.

Household   a group of people who share living accommodation. They are often families.

Roles   are expected patterns of behaviour. Age and gender are often the basis of family roles.

Functions   the functions of the family are the ways in which it helps to satisfy the needs of the social system, for example, the socialization of children.

Housework/domestic labour   the work involved in running a household and caring for children at home. It is usually carried out by women and is often unpaid.

Childhood   is the early stage of social life. It is socially constructed rather than biologically defined.

Old age   tends to be defined in modern society in terms of retirement from work and dependence. In pre-industrial societies it may be equated with wisdom and high status.

Nuclear family   consists of parents and their immature children. G. P. Murdock claimed that the nuclear family was *universal*.

Extended family   includes the additions to the nuclear family of other kin. They may be a third generation or the families of adult brothers or sisters.

Kinship   kin are a larger family group where relationships are based on 'blood' (perhaps we ought to say genes nowadays) or marriage. In many societies some relationships are seen as more important than others in defining rules of inheritance of property or incest.

► **Patrilineal kin** are traced through fathers
► **Matrilineal kin** are traced through mothers

Symmetrical family describes the tendency towards increased equality within the family. Functionalists talk of joint conjugal roles.

TOPIC OUTLINE

You will need to look at a variety of theories, studies and arguments covering the following four aspects.

1 **Definitions** of family and household. You will need to be able to distinguish the two, and to note the influence of ideology on definitions of the family, such as functionalist, feminist and new right views.
2 **Structure** of family and household, including nuclear, different types of extended family, single parent families and childless families. Note the influence of lifecycle on individual families and be aware of the influence of social change on the family as an institution.
3 **Roles** of parents, children and the old. Also consider gender roles.
   ► The functionalist view of roles

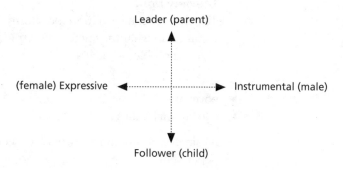

The (male) *instrumental* role in the view of functionalists involves working outside the home, whereas the (female) *expressive* role involves the provision of human companionship within the home. More up-to-date variants of the functionalist view of the family might include the *modern symmetrical family* (see Activity) and the *middle class (stage 4) family*, as defined by Willmott and Young, etc.
   ► The feminist view of roles emphasizes power which may be measured through the domestic division of labour, decision-making or even violence.
4 **Functions** of family for the wider society. A typical list includes:
   ► sexual, reproductive, legitimizing;
   ► socialization;
   ► economic: production and/or consumption;
   ► care and welfare; and
   ► affective.

The various ideological perspectives differ in the emphasis and interpretation they would put on such a list. For example, there are different views on socialization held by functionalists, Marxists, interactionists and feminists.

For each of these four aspects of the family – definitions, structure, roles and functions – you must consider:

▶ *Changes* related to urbanization, industrialization, secularization and the Welfare State;
▶ *Diversity* based on class, ethnicity and immigration; and
▶ *Disorganization* usefully defined by reference to role and functional failure. Consider domestic violence and the abuse of women, men, children and the old.

In each case change and diversity can be interpreted as the family being in decline or the family adapting to changing social conditions.

Many sociological debates can be seen in terms of agreeing or disagreeing with a rather idealized view of the family presented by some American functionalists.

Functionalists

Functionalists see one type of family as in the ascendancy. It is:

Modern, isolated, nuclear, egalitarian, with a reduced range of functions which fit the needs of individuals and society.

'Optimistic' functionalists, such as K. Davis, are even positive about rising divorce rates. These are seen as evidence that people have higher expectations of marriage and they are merely rejecting a particular relationship rather than the institution of marriage. This is why remarriage is common.

The new right

The new right have a more pessimistic view. They tend to be critical of any variation in what they perceive as traditional family values and blame all sorts of social problems, such as

▶ deviance
▶ poverty and
▶ educational failure,

on single parent families which are seen as dysfunctional and probably welfare dependent.

Marxists

Marxists share the view with functionalists that the modern family has developed in response to broader social change. However, they see the family as reproducing the relations of production in capitalist society rather than fitting the needs of industrial society.

Feminists

Feminists have a wide range of views on the modern family. In general they are critical of the family as an institution which enforces patriarchy.

REVISION ACTIVITY

The symmetrical family: Evidence and arguments

For   *Against*

Indicate whether the developments listed below support or refute the idea that a symmetrical family has developed in modern society. You can place the number of each development under the heading '*For*' or '*Against*'.

1 The family has become smaller.
2 Women take the main responsibility for home and children.

3 The family has become increasingly 'privatized' and home-centered.
4 The extended family provides support.
5 Conjugal roles have become more equal but are not the same.
6 Important decisions are made by men alone.
7 Men may be victims of domestic violence.
8 Men may help with the housework.
9 More women work in paid employment.
10 Men have become more work-centred and spend less time at home.
11 Women play expressive roles and men play instrumental roles.
12 Women are the head of the family.

 ## EXAMINATION QUESTIONS

Question 1

Item A

Some writers emphasize the cost effectiveness of the conjugal family in reproducing labour power. This argument is based on the assumption that unpaid domestic labour (that is, the labour of the housewife) lowers the minimum cost of labour to the advantage of capital. This because workers would have to buy in domestic and childcare services if the family did not exist. *5*
This would add to their living costs and raise wage levels. Other writers have suggested that the family not only secures unpaid domestic labour for capitalism but also provides a reserve army of labour. Housewives can be drawn upon in periods of high demand for labour and, when no longer needed, can return to the family without appearing in unemployment statistics. *10*

> *Source:* adapted from F. R. Elliot, *The Family: Change or Continuity*, (Macmillan)

Item B

Feminists argue that 'welfare' legislation has incorporated the patriarchal ideology of the society that originated it. Acts such as the Factory Acts of the nineteenth century, which were supposedly designed to protect women from working long hours in unsafe conditions, in fact were designed to take them out of the workforce and keep them in the home, no longer competing with *5*
men for jobs. The 1911 National Insurance Act insured male workers but excluded married women, who were thought to be the responsibility of their husband and dependent on him. The Beveridge Report adopted the same approach: 'the attitude of the housewife to gainful employment outside the home is not and should not be the same as that of the single woman. She has *10*
other duties'.

> *Source:* P. Trowler, *Investigating Health, Welfare and Poverty*, (Unwin Hyman)

Item C

Functionalists regard the family as an important 'organ' in the 'body' of society. It is what the family 'does' or the functions of the family that most interest them. For example, we can look at sex and reproduction. According to functionalists, marriage and the nuclear family provide the best opportunity for the socially controlled expression of the sex drive. More importantly, they *5*
provide the necessary institutional stability for the reproduction and nurturing (bringing up) of children. The bringing up of children requires considerable time and effort: human maturation takes longer than that of any other species relative to lifespan. To be brought up effectively, children usually require the help of more than one person (for practical if not emotional reasons). In most *10*
societies the two people who produce a child are expected to take responsibility for its upbringing.

> *Source:* M. O'Donnell, *New Introduction to Sociology*, (Nelson)

(a) Which sociological perspective is illustrated by *Item A*? *(1 mark)*
(b) Explain briefly what is meant by 'patriarchal ideology', (lines 1–2) *Item B*
    (2 marks)
(c) Item C states that 'in most societies, the two people who produce a child are
    expected to take responsibility for its upbringing' (lines 11–12). How far is
    this view supported by sociological evidence? *(5 marks)*
(d) Assess the contribution of feminist perspectives to an understanding of the
    family. *(8 marks)*
(e) *Items A and C* suggest very different views about the functions of the family
    in modern society. Discuss these points of view and assess their relative
    merits. *(9 marks)*

                                                             Total: 25 marks
                                                                (AEB, 1992)

Question 2

(a) Briefly explain what sociologists mean by the concept of the 'isolated
    nuclear family'. *(4 marks)*
(b) Identify two aspects of modern social life which are seen by some sociol-
    ogists as promoting the spread of the isolated nuclear family. *(4 marks)*
(c) What evidence is there for the view that extended kinship remains
    significant in the UK. *(7 marks)*
(d) Evaluate the view that the isolation of the nuclear family contributes to
    marital instability and high divorce rates. *(10 marks)*

                                                             Total: 25 marks
                                                                (IBS, 1995)

Question 3

Item A

The analysis of the family from a functionalist perspective involves three main
questions.

Firstly, 'What are the functions of the family?' Answers to this question deal
with the contributions made by the family to the maintenance of the social
system. It is assumed that society has certain functional prerequisites or basic   **5**
needs that must be met if it is to survive and operate efficiently.

A second and related question asks 'What are the functional relationships
between the family and other parts of the social system?' For example, the
family must be integrated to some extent with the economic system.

The third question is concerned with the functions performed by an   **10**
institution or part of society for the individual. In the case of the family, this
question considers the functions of the family for its individual members.

Increasingly, this picture of the family is coming under strong criticism.
Some observers are suggesting that, on balance, the family may well be
dysfunctional both for society and for its individual members. This criticism   **15**
has been directed mainly at the family in western industrial society.

Source: adapted from M. Haralambos, *Sociology: Themes and Perspectives* (1990),
                                                                Unwin-Hyman

Item B

The effects on children of a 'broken home' are greater where remarriage
occurs than if the children remain with a single parent. This is the rather
surprising conclusion to be drawn from research by the Family Policy Studies
Centre.

Those whose parents divorced and subsequently married other partners   **5**
became part of what is termed a 'stepfamily'. Dr Kathleen Kiernan, research
director at the FPSC, found from her research that those from stepfamilies
were:

▶ less likely to continue in education after age 16;

▶ less likely to do well in terms of work and careers;   *10*

▶ three times more likely than their counterparts to leave home before the age of 18;

▶ stepdaughters were twice as likely to leave school at age 16, were twice as likely to become mothers while still teenagers and four times as likely to marry aged under 20.   *15*

Source: adapted from M. Denscombe, *Sociology Update* (1992)

Item C

Marxists focus on the ways in which the family has sustained class inequalities and patterns of exploitation. This is, in part, a recognition of the way in which privilege and inequality are passed on from generation to generation (e.g. through inheritance, educational advantages or through the 'cultural capital' provided by the home) but more the way in which class relationships are   *5* reproduced over time. If we are to understand how capitalism – or any system, come to that – persists over time, it is important to look at the family and household. The family, along with the educational system, is often seen as an institution centrally concerned with the passing on of values such as belief in free enterprise and competition, individualism and taken-for-granted   *10* assumptions about the natures of women and men.

Source: adapted from David Morgan, *The Family, in Developments in Sociology,* Vol. 1, Causeway

(a) What do sociologists mean by 'functional prerequisites' (*Item A* line 5) and 'cultural capital' (*Item C* line 4)? *(2 marks)*

(b) Suggest **two** sociological reasons why Dr Kiernan's results are seen as surprising by the author of *Item B*. *(2 marks)*

(c) Assess the contribution of the functionalist approach identified in *Item A* to an understanding of the modern industrial family. *(8 marks)*

(d) How far do you agree with the argument in *Item C* (lines 1–2) that 'the family has sustained class inequalities and patterns of exploitation'? *(6 marks)*

(e) What have sociologists identified as the 'taken-for-granted assumptions about the natures of women and men' (*Item C* lines 10–11) and how have these assumptions been criticized? *(7 marks)*

Total: 25 marks
(AEB, 1994)

Education

Keep your notes up-to-date. There have been some major developments in the sociology of education which sometimes contradict previous research. This does not mean the older research was 'wrong' but it does indicate that things have changed.

You can keep up-to-date by:

▶ referring to press reports of current research. CD-ROM in your school or local library will help;
▶ looking at recent articles in journals such as *Sociology Update* or *Sociology Review*;
▶ attending conferences aimed at A-level students; and
▶ looking at the latest possible edition of textbooks.

If you cannot gain access to the latest material, do not despair. Use your sociological skills to question whether older research is still valid. This is valued by examiners in all topic areas. For example, you can evaluate previous research that explains the relative failure of girls in schools by referring to widely publicized evidence that girls now gain better results in public examinations.

Don't worry if you feel you don't know everything
Neither do your examiners. You only have a limited time to respond to questions. It is worth remembering that the AEB data-response questions only allocate 5 out of 25 marks to knowledge and understanding, as you are expected to use the knowledge given in the items.

Key words and their definitions

Curriculum   the sum of learning experiences offered by schools.

Hidden curriculum   that which is learned in school which is not part of the official curriculum. Values and beliefs are reinforced by the organization of the school as well as by what is learned in class.

Meritocracy   a system where rewards depend on merit: that is, ability and effort, and not on ascribed characteristics.

Vocational education   work-related learning. Either specific training or preparation for employment in general.

Self-fulfilling prophecy   a prediction which helps bring about what was expected. When applied to education it suggests that pupils who are expected to succeed will do well because of the effects of this prediction.

Cultural deprivation   the adverse effects of the 'inferior' culture – values and beliefs – of some homes on childrens' educational achievements.

Material deprivation   the adverse effects of low income and poor housing on childrens' educational achievements.

TOPIC OUTLINE

1 Differential educational achievement

Organize your revision and answers using a general framework of explanations. The following headings may be useful:

- ▶ **innate ability**
- ▶ **out-of-school factors**
  - (1) material factors
  - (2) cultural factors
- ▶ **in-school factors**
  - (1) the education system
  - (2) the school
  - (3) teacher–pupil interaction

You can apply these types of explanation to differences in educational achievement occurring between:

- ▶ **social classes;**
- ▶ **gender groups**; and
- ▶ **ethnic groups**.

Not all explanations are equally relevant for these different social groups. For example, material deprivation is more significant in explaining different educational achievement via class inequalities than via gender inequalities.

Definitions of *social class*, *gender* and *ethnicity* are all problematic. They are socially defined and their meanings are socially constructed.

2 The role and functions of education

You should be able to identify and discuss different sociological views on *the relationship between education and the wider society*. The following theoretical approaches should be critically assessed:

Marxist
Education, involving both institutions and ideas, is seen as part of the superstructure of capitalist society. Bowles and Gintis offer a clear view of the relationship between education, work and the family.

Bowles and Gintis
In a series of empirical and theoretical studies of schooling in the USA, Bowles and Gintis developed their *correspondence* theory of education. They argue that there are interdependent relationships between the family, education and work. Examples of the correspondence between schools and work include:

1. The fragmentation and stratification of school knowledge is similar to deskilled and fragmented work.
2. Pupils rely on teachers for knowledge, as workers rely on managers.
3. Both school and workplace motivate and control through extrinsic rewards.
4. Pupils learn to be submissive to authority.
5. Both school and workplace are hierarchically organized.
6. Rewards appear to be based on merit, which thereby legitimizes inequality.

Functionalism
Education is related to the wider society by its functions which satisfy the needs of the social system for integration, adaptation and social control.

Durkheim

Durkheim saw education as the methodological socialization of the young. It provided them with the general qualities necessary to be members of a society and with the specific skills to fill particular occupational roles. Thus education systems contribute towards satisfying the functional needs of integration, social control and role allocation.

Feminism

Identifies the role of education as reproducing patriarchy, both through the curriculum and the organization of the school.

Relevant studies

Deem (1980) showed how girls were encouraged into 'feminine', and thus low-status, subjects by the school. Blackstone (1980) showed how girls were allowed to avoid science in mixed school, but to a lesser extent in single-sex schools. Oakley (1982) suggested that the hidden curriculum was a reflection, rather than a cause, of women's position in society.

Teacher–pupil interaction is a significant factor according to Wolpe (1977), who wrote that girls were 'taught' to smile at male teachers, to be passive and to develop self-discipline earlier than boys. Delamont (1980) showed how different expectations began in nursery school, and in a subsequent study showed how the YTS pushed girls into feminine jobs. Stanworth (1983) reported that teachers were more likely to know the boys' names and to interact with them in class, whereas they underestimated the abilities and ambitions of girls.

The New Right

Would like to see educational resources distributed on free market principles. They also yearn for what are perceived as traditional values in the curriculum and teaching methods, although this may be incompatible with what the 'consumer' wants.

The four approaches examined above should be applied to issues such as the relationships between:

▶ Education and the **economy**;
▶ Education and **inequality**;
▶ Education and **social control**; and
▶ Education and **cultural reproduction**.

In each case you should consider both:

▶ *Educational institutions*, such as the hierarchical organization of schools; and
▶ *Ideas/ideologies*, such as the formal curriculum and the hidden curriculum. The hidden curriculum includes:

  – *Attitudes and ideas* which are taught informally or found in the way textbooks are written.
  – *Organization of the school or college.* This may itself be a source of learning for pupils. Most organizations are based on a hierarchy, where people at the top exercise authority over those below.
  – *Rules.* Teachers are seen to control both time and space. Pupils may not be allowed to pass time unless it is on an approved activity. Teachers may refer to classrooms as 'my room' and many spaces are denied to pupils altogether. Toilets are often seen by pupils as a refuge from teacher authority but even this space is open to teacher inspection. There may also be rules about students' appearance and conduct out of school as well as in school.

— *The relationships between teachers and pupils*, and between pupils themselves. As described above, these may reinforce attitudes on gender and race.
— *Competition*. In both academic and sports activities, competition may be seen as part of a hidden curriculum. Of course in some cases competition may be discussed openly and become part of the official curriculum.

Ensure that you understand the evidence and arguments about the *major social and political issues in education*, such as:

1 Selective or comprehensive schools;
2 Vocational training;
3 Religion and schools;
4 The expansion of higher education;
5 The National Curriculum and testing;
6 Increased nursery provision; and
7 Spending on education.

Once again, it is not detailed knowledge that's required but the ability to analyse changes using sociological concepts and the ability to use the evidence to evaluate sociological approaches.

The similarities and differences between political parties on these issues can be explored. The new right commitment to the free market can be compared with the Social Democratic attempts to reform through local and central government planning.

All political parties currently seem committed to the idea that education should be an engine of economic growth through training.

REVISION ACTIVITY

Identify *three* similarities and *three* differences between Marxist and functionalist explanations of the role of education in society.

EXAMINATION QUESTIONS

Question 1
(a) Briefly explain what is meant by the concept of 'cultural capital'. *(4 marks)*
(b) Identify *two* examples of skills and knowledge outside the formal curriculum that may contribute to educational success. *(4 marks)*
(c) Outline how material factors might explain class differences in educational attainment. *(7 marks)*
(d) Assess the relative importance of cultural and material factors in sociological explanations of educational attainment. *(10 marks)*

Total: 25 marks
(IBS Specimen paper)

Question 2

Item A
The role of the teacher as an agent of social control is extremely important in assessing the role of the hidden curriculum in maintaining gender inequality. Obviously, teachers' attitudes towards the role of education for women and men will influence their relationship with students. Spender found that in mixed classrooms, boys received two-thirds of the teacher time, benefitting from the teacher's attention and distracting from the amount of time spent with the girls.

Just as the attitudes of teachers can play a role in reinforcing gender

5

inequalities through the hidden curriculum so can the attitudes and behaviour
of the students. Jones highlights the high level of sexual violence initiated by   **10**
boys in mixed schools against females, both students and teachers. Jones
argues that school is a system for legitimating male violence against women
and for making this violence seem part of everyday life.

Source: Kate Reynolds, 'Feminist thinking on education'
Social Studies Review, Vol. 6, no. 4

Item B
Schools can make a difference
Although most people remain in the class they were born in, about one in
three working-class children move up the social scale and about the same
proportion of middle- and lower-middle move down. Individual intelligence is
one reason that partly explains upward movement, and going to a good school
is another. But what is a good school?   **5**
   Michael Rutter's study *Fifteen Thousand Hours* examined this problem. Rutter
and his team looked at only twelve Inner London secondary schools so it is
important not to over-generalize their findings. Rutter's research is
summarized below:

Factors measured	*Teachers' qualities linked with success in these four areas*
	Teachers who are:
Attendance	
Academic achievement	Punctual
Behaviour in school	Well-organized
Rate of delinquency outside school	Patient
	Encouraging
	Inspiring
	Willing to share extra-curricular activities with pupils
	Consistent

Source: M. O'Donnell and J. Garrod, *Sociology in Practice*, Nelson

Item C
The Self-fulfilling Prophecy
When pupils come into a school, teachers make judgements on their ability,
based on many different things. These labels are, for example, 'bright', 'able',
'thick', 'less able', 'practical', 'academic', etc. However, these labels are not
neutral, nor do they describe the real possibilities of students, but are based on
commonsense knowledge of what type of student is 'good' and which 'bad'.
Thus it has been shown that teachers have stereotypes linked to class ('from
broken homes'), gender ('she's just a girl'), race ('West Indians are noisy') and
even physical attractiveness ('snotty-nosed kid'). Teachers then act towards
students on the basis of such stereotypes – for example, those students who are
labelled 'bright' are given more time to answer questions than those who are
seen as unlikely to know the answer anyway.

Source: adapted from Tony Lawson, 'Sociology: a conceptual approach',
Checkmate

(a) What does Jones suggest is the way in which schools 'legitimate male
     violence' (Item A)? *(1 mark)*
(b) Identify *both* factors which *Item B* suggests contribute to upward social
     mobility. *(1 mark)*
(c) The concept of the self-fulfilling prophecy described in *Item C* has been

criticized by some sociologists. Identify *three* ways in which the concept might be criticized. *(3 marks)*

(d) Using information from the *Items* and elsewhere, evaluate sociological contributions to an understanding of the hidden curriculum, as it affects *female* pupils. *(10 marks)*

(e) Assess the extent to which school factors, such as those identified in the *Items*, explain differential educational achievement between *social classes*. *(10 marks)*

Total: 25 marks
(AEB, 1993)

Question 3

Item A

There are two obvious ways in which teachers' judgements of pupils may have an impact on the social distribution of achievement. First, as several studies have shown, teachers' expectations can colour their assessment of pupils' performance; in Goodacre's study, infant school teachers rated children whom they thought came from a middle-class background as better able to read than those whom they believed to be from working-class homes; standardized tests did not, however, reveal such a marked difference in the reading level of these two groups of children. In cases such as this, teachers' assessments of pupils reflect their views of what middle-class and other pupils should be capable of, rather than their actual performance. Second, teachers may, because of low expectations, make fewer attempts to stimulate pupils or to overcome areas of weakness.

Source: adapted from Bilton *et al.*, *Introductory Sociology*

Item B

All the factors which produce poor school progress from working-class children also affect children from West Indian and many Asian homes. This is hardly surprising as the majority of these children are from working-class homes. But there are some problems which are faced only by children from ethnic minority backgrounds. For some of these children, the main language of the home may not be English. So their studies are carried out, to some extent, in a 'foreign' language. Although West Indian children speak English at home, it may be in a dialect that differs from standard English.

It is rare for teachers to be openly racist but cultural differences and poor performance in some IQ tests by black children have created the belief in some teachers' minds that black children are more likely to be slow learners. This can influence the way that teachers label black pupils and so retard their progress.

Source: adapted from Stephen Moore, *Sociology Alive*

Item C

Under-achievement meant that equality of opportunity was not ensured by the schooling system for a variety of reasons. Evidence was advanced to show that children of equal ability had a better or worse chance of obtaining an education suited to their talents, depending on their social background. In particular, children from a semi- or unskilled manual working-class home did less well than their ability as measured in tests of intelligence would indicate. In other words, social class and background affected achievement.

Source: adapted from M. Davies and B. King, *Discovering Sociology*

Item D

One of the reasons for introducing comprehensive education was that, with mixed ability teaching and by offering a new curriculum, comprehensive schools would offer 'equality of opportunity for all' and not reward class background. However, comprehensive education has come under attack recently. Some critics argue that it has 'lowered standards' (though it is difficult to know what is meant by this) and believe that the tripartite system should be restored. Others have argued that many comprehensives were large and inefficient. It has also been argued that many comprehensives retained streaming and therefore recreated the 'tripartite system under one roof'.

(a) According to *Item C*, from which social groups did children who under-achieve come? *(1 mark)*

(b) Evaluate sociological explanations of the 'poor school progress' made by some children from West Indian and Asian homes (*Item B*). *(8 marks)*

(c) To what extent do you agree that teachers' judgements of pupils are the main cause of under-achievement in schools? Refer to the *Items* and other evidence in your answer. *(8 marks)*

(d) With reference to the *Items* and elsewhere, asses the view that the introduction of comprehensive schools has led to 'equal opportunity for all'. *(8 marks)*

Total: 25 marks
(AEB, 1994)

4 Social stratification

The study of *stratification* and *differentiation* is an essential part of your A-level or AS-level course. You will need to prepare for specific questions on stratification (this is compulsory in the IBS syllabus) and also be able to apply your knowledge and understanding of the theories and studies of stratification to virtually every other topic you choose.

You must be familiar with your syllabus and with past questions in order to identify the most likely themes of questions. Because of the rather daunting amount of sociology that could be examined in this section, the 1998 AEB syllabus has moved some potential stratification questions to other parts of the syllabus.

The distribution of income and wealth is examined under the heading of 'Wealth, Welfare and Poverty' and the cultural aspects of class, gender, ethnicity and age are examined in the new 'Culture and identity' section of the syllabus.

When revising other topics, take note of those (frequent) questions that examine social inequalities.

Keywords and their definitions

Stratification   the division of society into a more or less permanent hierarchy based on social characteristics. Stratification is a form of inequality that limits the opportunity of groups to acquire rewards.

Social class   the form of stratification found in capitalist societies. The class hierarchy is defined in economic terms: wealth, income, occupation are often involved. Social class is defined, measured and explained in a variety of ways.

Social status   a Weberian concept describing the prestige given to groups by other members of society. It can often be seen in the consumption patterns or lifestyle of the group. Weber distinguished social status from class, although they may coincide.

Social mobility   refers to the movement up or down the class structure by individuals or groups.

Underclass   a class at the bottom of the system of social stratification, beneath and separate from the working class. The term, once used mainly by Weberians, has developed a new meaning when used by the new right.

Reserve army of labour   a Marxist concept describing groups who are available for work when required by employers during labour shortages but are not seen as entitled to work when unemployment rises.

Gender   refers to socially defined differences between men and women. It is distinguished from sex which describes biological differences.

Patriarchy   a system of social inequality where men dominate women, both in society as a whole and within the family.

Ethnicity   refers to a distinctive cultural identity accepted by a group and/or attributed to them by others. Ethnicity may be related to race.

Race   perceived biological differences which are given a social meaning and may be the basis of a system of stratification. The concept of race has little biological validity when applied to humans.

TOPIC OUTLINE

General advice

There is such a broad range of evidence and arguments that could be used to answer questions that it is necessary to try to identify theories and studies that can be used in a variety of questions.

You should also practise doing past questions. Three techniques which may help are:

▶ interpreting and applying evidence and arguments involving stratification from the *Items* presented in data response questions (look carefully at the *Items* in Questions 1–3 below);
▶ practising applying theoretical perspectives, which you can learn in advance, to these questions; and
▶ using previously learned general criticisms to apply to specific questions.

For example, in questions on ethnic inequality, you can raise the problems of analysing evidence involving the existence of differences *between* various ethnic groups and differences *within* an ethnic group based on gender, class and age.

1 Theories of social class

You must be able to outline and assess the strengths and weaknesses of these theories:

▶ **Marxist**
▶ **Weberian**
▶ **Functionalist**

Some basic questions may help you to distinguish between the theories:

▶ How is social class defined?
▶ How many classes are there?
▶ How is the class system likely to develop?

Below is an example of how you can apply these questions to *Marxist* theory.

Example: *Marx' view of stratification*
1 Class is based on ownership of the means of production.
2 There are only two significant classes: the *bourgeoisie* who own the means of production (such as factories) and the *proletariat* who are the class of wage labourers working in the factories and generally living in towns.
3 The relationship between classes is based on exploitation and oppression.
4 The working class (proletariat) is subjugated by both physical and ideological control.
5 Economic laws will lead to the development of class conflict. Marx predicts:
    ▶ Monopolization of capital
    ▶ Homogenization of the working class
    ▶ Pauperization of the working class
    ▶ Polarization of the two classes
6 Class conflict will lead to revolution, the triumph of the working class and the development of a classless society.

Changes in the class structure

The following issues need examination. Consider whether changes have occurred and, if so, identify their causes and consequences.

In each case you should try to compare and contrast the Marxist and Weberian approaches to the issue.

1 Embourgeoisement
2 A fragmented working class
3 The underclass
4 Proletarianization
5 A fragmented middle class
6 A classless society

Figure 2 demonstrates some of the essential features of the class structure as perceived by Marx and Weber.

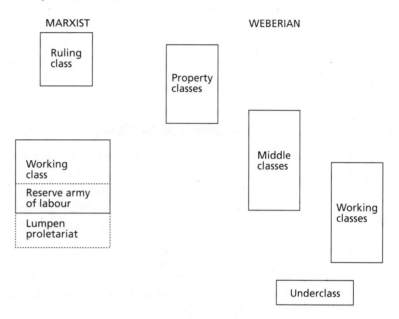

Figure 2: The class structure of capitalist societies

The Marxist model shows two classes. There is no separate class beneath the working class, although Marx's concept of a lumpen proletariat can sound very like a new right view of the underclass. Weaker sections of the working class (perhaps identified by age, gender or ethnicity) may form a reserve army of labour *within* the working class.

The Weberian model also indicates an upper class defined in terms of ownership. However, rather than a single class, there are divisions based on how much property is owned. Similarly, the non-owning classes are divided on the basis of market situation and work situation into a number of middle (white collar) and working classes (manual workers). Beneath the working class is a separate and distinct underclass.

You can try to produce similar diagrammatic models of:

▶ Functionalist theory – a pyramid without distinct class boundaries?
▶ Embourgeoisement – a diamond or onion shape with a swollen middle class?

2 Age stratification

Age is a social construction. The extent to which it forms the basis of a system of stratification is culturally and historically specific. Examine inequality by looking at the following age groups:

Childhood

Children can be seen as lacking legal and political rights. They are subject to exploitation and the abuse of power in the family, school and labour market.

Hood-Williams (1990) used the term 'age patriarchy' to describe the disadvantaged position of children.

Youth

Youth can also be seen as a disadvantaged age group in the family, school and labour market. They are also perceived as a social problem. For example, youth unemployment is seen not just as a problem for the young jobless but as a threat to social order.

Adults

Adults are seen as 'normal'. They are frequently neglected in studies of age.

The old

Conventionally the old are seen as enjoying high social status in simple societies and low status, based on dependency, in modern societies.

In Britain the old comprise a significant proportion of those who are dependent on benefits, yet they are rarely considered to be part of an underclass.

3 Gender stratification

Inequality tends to be studied in the fields of:

Gender, sex and sexuality

Be aware of the social construction of gender and the significance of gender, sex and sexuality in creating and reinforcing inequality.

The family

Be able to discuss the unequal division of labour and power associated with the housewife–mother role. Consider children as well as adults in the family.

The labour market

Be able to evaluate explanations of women's position including the Marxist reserve army of labour, the underclass, the gendered labour market and the dual labour market.

Note: the three fields are inter-related.

In addition to showing a critical understanding of the main assumptions of feminism in general, you should be able to evaluate some major strands of feminist thinking such as:

► Marxist feminism;
► radical feminism; and
► liberal feminism.

4 Ethnic inequality

The relationship between stratification and ethnicity/race can be examined from the following perspectives:

Marxist

Ethnic inequality is seen as relatively unimportant.

Ethnic divisions within the working class inhibit the development of class consciousness.

Racism is an ideology which is part of the superstructure of capitalist societies.

Weberian

Ethnic inequality is seen as the result of differences in power dependent on class, status and power.

Racism is not the cause of the development of an underclass but the basis of the allocation of workers to the lowest levels of the labour market.

Functionalist

This has the most optimistic view. Immigration serves a valuable economic function (e.g. meeting labour shortages) but may be the basis of a temporary threat to social order. Minorities will, however, accept consensual values and eventually be integrated into the wider society.

The arguments over the existence of an ethnically differentiated underclass are a common focus of questions.

The application of theories of inequality to the difference types of social inequality and other topics

Theory of inequality	Type of inequality				Other topics
	Class	Gender	Ethnicity	Age	
Functionalist	✓	✓	✓	✓	Wealth, Poverty and Welfare (WPW) Education Development
Marxist	✓	✓	✓ (Reserve army of labour)	✓	All
Weberian underclass	✓		✓	✓	WPW
New right underclass	✓	✓ (Single mothers and young men)	✓	✓	WPW Family
Gendered labour market		✓			Family Education Work
Dual labour market	✓	✓ (Also core and periphery and flexible workforce)	✓	✓	Family Education Work

The ticks indicate that the theory can be used to explain a particular type of inequality. For example, weaker gender or ethnic groups may be more likely to become a reserve army of labour.

REVISION ACTIVITY

Produce sociological evidence and/or arguments that challenge these Marxist points of view.

1 Inequality is based solely on class differences.
2 Class depends on ownership of the means of production.
3 There are only two significant classes.
4 Profit and wealth derive from economic exploitation.
5 Economic 'laws' will lead to the development of class consciousness and class conflict.

6 Marx predicted:
- ► Monopolization of capital;
- ► Homogenization of the working class;
- ► Pauperization of the working class; and
- ► Polarization of the two classes.

7 Class conflict will lead to revolution, the triumph of the working class and the development of a classless society.

Hints:

- ► look first to Weber, then other theories such as functionalism, feminism, the new right, market liberalism;
- ► refer to the changes in the class structure listed above, such as embourgeoisement; and
- ► refer to current political and economic developments, if you follow the news, such as the rise and fall of the USSR.

EXAMINATION QUESTIONS

Question 1

Item A

Stratification is the division of a society or group into hierarchically ordered layers or strata. Among the main criteria by which people tend to be stratified are social class and status.

    The division of society into strata is often compared to geological formations. However, to compare social stratification to layers of rocks suggests   *5*
more rigidity in social structure than is usually found. If we remind ourselves that the relationship between geological strata can shift and change, the analogy begins to tell us more about the dynamic relationship between the social strata. Further, just as in certain cases where there is extreme tension between geological strata an earthquake can occur and change the structure of   *10*
the land, extreme social conflict, in the form of revolution, can overturn a given form of social stratification.

> *Source:* adapted from Mike O'Donnell, *A New Introduction to Sociology*, (1992), Thomas Nelson

Item B

Many feminists have long felt that not all women share the same struggle, and that working-class women have very different lives and different concerns from those of middle-class and upper-class women. Yet when they turn to the most fully theorized analysis of class – Marxism – they find that it devotes almost all its attention to men and male institutions. Indeed, in traditional Marxist   *5*
theories of social class, it was assumed that the interests of females were identical to those of men, and/or that men represented the interests of women more than adequately. Imagine a theory of social stratification which accepted women as independent and equal members of a household, rather than as class-dependent mothers and wives! *(5 marks)*   *10*

> *Source:* adapted from R. Warhol and D. R. Herndl (Eds), *Feminisms: an Anthology of Literary Theory and Criticism* (1992), Macmillan

Item C

Writers such as Charles Murray have developed the notion of the 'underclass', which has become increasingly fashionable in both the USA and this country too, and not just with the 'New Right'. It is used freely by the media, often as if

it were synonymous with poor people generally, with ethnic minorities and
with those seen as simply having 'dropped out of society'. It is, I would argue, a   **5**
dangerous concept. People tend to use it to mean what they want it to mean.
The language of the 'underclass' is not only imprecise, it is also disturbing; it is
the language of disease and contamination. Language such as this encourages
a pathological image of the groups of people mentioned above as being
somehow different from other people and to be feared. In effect, the term   **10**
'underclass' is so value-laden and emotive that it stigmatizes those included in
it as a group apart.

Source: adapted from Ruth Lister, 'Concepts of poverty', *Social Studies Review,*
Vol. 6, no. 5, May 1991

(a) What does Lister mean by a 'pathological image of the groups of people
    mentioned above' (*Item C, line 9*)? *(1 mark)*
(b) Identify *one* form of social stratification, other than social class, and briefly
    describe its main characteristics (*Item A*). *(4 marks)*
(c) What sociological evidence can be presented to support the claim made in
    Item B that theories of social stratification have ignored the existence of
    women? *(5 marks)*
(d) With reference to the Items and other sources, evaluate the Marxist
    account of class conflict. *(7 marks)*
(e) How far does sociological evidence support the idea that an 'underclass' has
    emerged in Britain *(Item C)*? *(8 marks)*

Total: 25 marks
(AEB, 1996)

Question 2

Item A

The persistence of racial and sexual discrimination is severe enough for some
to suggest that ethnic minorities, women and perhaps certain other groups
constitute an underclass. Giddens suggested that, in advanced capitalist
societies, a division was opening up between the working class and a growing
underclass. As separate groups, each would tend to develop different forms of   **5**
consciousness and action in pursuit of its interests. Similarly, Rex and
Tomlinson have argued that clear differences of life chances exist between
ethnic minorities and whites. Given increasing racism among whites and the
absence of any community-wide organizations, they concluded that 'the
greatest likelihood is that conflict in the community will grow'.   **10**

   Marxists are more reluctant to talk of an underclass. The study by Castles
and Kosack of migrant workers in Europe, for example, concludes that ethnic
minorities comprise 'a lower stratum of the working class', a 'reserve army of
labour' lacking citizenship rights. Like underclass theorists, however, Marxists
agree that ethnic minorities still constitute a 'replacement population',   **15**
employed (if at all) in non-skilled manual work.

   Among the top one-third of men with jobs, racial inequality has diminished
markedly. Among the bottom third, the opposite is true: the socioeconomic
profiles of whites and ethnic minorities remain distinct and an earnings gap
has opened up in manual work. There has been a class polarization both   **20**
within and between ethnic minority groups. In view of such diversity, it is not
surprising that a shared 'colour consciousness' and sense of the need for united
black action has failed to develop.

Source: adapted from A. Pilkington, 'Is there a British underclass?'
Sociology Review, February 1992

Item B

Domesticity is a defining feature of women's situation. As a consequence of industrialization, the home means 'family' rather than 'work' and the family means women. The modern housewife has a dual personality: she is both acting out a feminine role, and she is a worker involved in an occupation which has all the characteristics of other work roles except one: it is unpaid.   **5**

Housewives are sharply aware of the fact that responsibility for getting the work done is theirs. Some husbands will not carry the shopping bag for fear of being labelled 'effeminate'. 'If I'm changing a nappy, he runs out of the room, it makes him sick. He thinks it's my duty.' (Ex-fashion model, married to a retail chemist.)   **10**

The net effect of these traditional gender-role stereotypes, along with social-structural factors which maintain women's domesticity, is a pressure on women to become psychologically involved with housework. Some become 'obsessive' and 'houseproud', but what these terms really describe is a set of social values: the stereotype of housework as trivial, inferior work, the   **15**
view of women as neurotically preoccupied with unimportant matters, and the low social esteem in which women's traditional pursuits are held.

More working-class than middle-class housewives have a traditional orientation to housework (in which the housewife role is central to the self-concept) but, despite these differences, they all have to contend with the   **20**
daily experience of doing housework. Most named housework as the worst aspect of being a housewife. Others mentioned isolation, loneliness and constant domestic responsibility.

'Housework is hard, but my husband doesn't say that at all. I think he's wrong, because I'm going all the time. When his job's finished, it's finished   **25**
… Sunday he can lie in bed till twelve, get up, get dressed, and go for a drink, but my job never changes.' (Ex-factory worker, married to a driver's mate.)

Source: adapted from A. Oakley, *Housewife*, (1974)

(a) Give two examples of the lack of citizenship rights which may be experienced by members of ethnic minority groups (see *Item A*, line 14). *(2 marks)*

(b) Give two reasons why 'more working-class than middle-class housewives have a traditional orientation to housework' (see *Item B*, lines 18–19). *(2 marks)*

(c) Assess sociological explanations of the housewife role. *(11 marks)*

(d) Drawing on material from *Item A* and elsewhere, assess the view that an ethnically distinct underclass exists in Britain. *(10 marks)*

Total: 25 marks
(AEB, 1994)

Question 3

Item A

At the root of our confusion about class is our equation of class with money. As we have become more prosperous, as the working classes got their washing machines in the sixties and videos in the eighties, old class allegiances have faded. Everyone moved on up. We may have not gone fully into Europe, but Europe has got fully into us. Cappuccino, fresh pasta and good wine are now   **5**
available almost everywhere. We are all middle class now – or so the myth goes.

Clearly, class is no longer a fashionable concept, but the uncomfortable truth is that the gap between the classes is widening. We may be in danger of losing

the statistics that show, time and time again, that members of the working class   **10**
are far more likely to die of heart disease, lung cancer and strokes than the
middle class. Or that babies born to middle-class parents have a better chance
of survival than those born to working-class ones. For, in the end, class is not
just a question of style or even lifestyle, but of life itself.

Source: Suzanne Moore, 'The ups and downs of Them and Us', *Observer*,
6 October 1991

Item B
A study of the middle class argues that 'decomposition', or, to use the author's
term, 'fragmentation', is occurring to this group. Roberts *et al.* examine the
'class images' of a wide range of white-collar employees. They conclude that a
variety of class images occur and that this is indicative of the fragmentation of
the middle class into various strata. Accordingly, it is no longer accurate to talk   **5**
of *the* middle class.

Source: adapted from M. O'Donnell, *A New Introduction to Sociology*
(1992), Nelson

Item C
Herbert Gans, sociologist and writer on the relation between class and plural
cultures, suggests five 'taste cultures' and while these caricature the situation,
as all social categories must do, they also reveal the variety of values. At the top
of the hierarchy sits the high culture of the avante-garde, the cutting edge, the
modernists and postmodernists. Just below this is traditional high culture, or   **5**
upper-class country culture: country houses and the nostalgia industry, the
gentry and what remains of aristocratic culture. Then there is the classless
middle-class taste culture: large and formless, a compromise of all the others.
Below that is the conjunction of the lower middle-class and upper working-
class: vital and vulgar. Finally, there is the underclass, the bottom ten per cent   **10**
which exists in a culture of poverty and dependency, overlooked by the rest of
society and without a culture industry to target them.

Source: adapted from Charles Jencks, 'Leap-frogging the cultural pyramid',
Guardian, 16 January 1992

(a) Which class culture does *Item C* suggest is 'classless'? *(1 mark)*
(b) Apart from the ways mentioned in *Item A*, suggest one other way in which
    the working class may be disadvantaged compared to the middle class.
    (1 mark)
(c) How far does sociological evidence support the view that the 'gap between
    the classes is widening' (*Item A line 9*)? *(7 marks)*
(d) To what extent do sociologists agree that the modern class structure is
    fragmented (*Item B*)? Refer to the *Items* and other sources in your answer.
    (8 marks)
(e) Assess the usefulness of the concept 'underclass' (*Item C*) in describing the
    social position of women. *(8 marks)*

Total: 25 marks
(AEB, 1995)

5 Poverty, welfare and social policy

Although poverty is usually identified as a distinct topic at A-level it is wise not to study it in isolation from other areas of the syllabus.

It is very helpful to have a clear understanding of *social differentiation and stratification*. For many sociologists the study of poverty is an integral part of the study of stratification. The poor are those who are at the bottom of the social hierarchy and the reasons for poverty are the explanations of inequality.

You need to understand stratification to succeed in most questions, so you should try to gain the maximum benefit from your revision by examining the contribution of *Marxist, Weberian, functionalist* and *feminist theories of inequality* to an understanding of poverty. Similarly, you will find concepts such as the underclass and *reserve army of labour* useful.

Remember
The study of poverty is an ideological activity: the values of researchers are influential in determining the ways in which poverty is defined, measured and explained.

Key words and their definitions

Poverty   does not have a generally accepted sociological definition.

Absolute poverty   means lacking the basic necessities of life. Health and even life itself is threatened.

Relative poverty   exists when people earn so much less than average pay that they are unable to participate in ordinary living patterns.

Subjective poverty   is the feeling of being left out of everyday life because of lack of money.

The culture of poverty   is a set of values, norms and behaviour patterns that distinguish the poor from the rest of society.

The Welfare State   describes government intervention in society to deal with social problems and provide social services for all. The main services are health, education, social security and housing.

Social problems   are issues of public concern. Sociologists have conflicting views on who defines social problems. They may be objectively defined or socially constructed.

Sociological problems   are questions that sociologists wish to explain.

Social policy   is the ideology that underlies the management of social institutions in order to achieve particular societal goals. The most discussed aspects of social policy include State health, education and welfare provision.

TOPIC OUTLINE

1 The Welfare State

What is the Welfare State? You should be able to:

▶ explain how the government uses its power to modify market forces by:
  1 ensuring a minimum family income;
  2 tackling the effects of problems such as sickness, retirement and unemployment; and
  3 offering social services to all.
▶ explain and evaluate a variety of sociological approaches to social policy and the Welfare State:
  1 **social democratic reformist social policy**;
  2 **the functionalist approach**;
  3 **Marxists**;
  4 **the market liberals or the new right**; and
  5 **feminists**.
▶ examine the extent to which the Welfare State reduces inequality and in particular redistributes resources between the rich and poor. As seen above there are five different ideological viewpoints on this.
▶ assess the effects of:
  1 **taxation**; and
  2 **benefits**.

It will be useful in your revision if for each of these sociological approaches, you highlight the main aspects of the approach and list criticisms derived from the other viewpoints. An example is provided in the text below.

Example Social democratic reformist social policy
This has been proposed by many social democratically included British sociologists. They include T. H. Marshall and R. Titmus, writing in the early days of the post-war Welfare State, and P. Townsend, who has been influential in discussions on poverty, welfare and health issues for the last 30 years. Such writers have suggested that the Welfare State is, at least potentially, the solution to poverty by providing a safety net for those who are temporarily or permanently unable to support themselves. They believe that all citizens have a right to basic levels of welfare provision including education, health services and pensions, and that these should be universally provided.

Critics

1 The market liberals from the new right are critical of the increasing cost of providing universal welfare benefits, the alleged unfairness of supporting 'scroungers' and the debilitating effect which State support is thought to have on its recipients, i.e. the creation of a culture of dependency.
2 Marxists see the gains as an illusion which fails to redistribute income or as a successful safety valve to dampen down protest or maintain 'false consciousness'.
3 Feminists see the existing structure of the Welfare State as perpetuating the subjugation of women via the system of taxation/benefits supporting a family household structure which maintains patriarchy.

---

2 The problems of defining and measuring poverty

Defining poverty is both a political and a sociological problem. Definitions and explanations of poverty often reflect the ideological views of writers.

You must be able to define and discuss the usefulness of different definitions of poverty including:

Absolute poverty

Explain Rowntree's concepts of:

▶ primary poverty;
▶ secondary poverty; and
▶ the cycle of poverty.

Criticize absolute definitions of poverty:

▶ The distinction between necessities and luxuries is historically and culturally specific.
▶ There may be *cultural* as well as material characteristics of poverty.

Relative poverty

Explain the development of the concept of relative poverty. Refer to Townsend and his critics.

The poverty line is based on what is needed to take part in everyday life and comparisons with average earnings are often made.

Criticize relative definitions of poverty:

▶ Those who lack items may do so by choice not because of lack of means.
▶ Cultural needs may change.
▶ Poverty may appear to describe inequality or even envy rather than real deprivation.

3 Explanations of poverty

The major theme in questions is often evaluating competing *explanations of poverty*.

The first three explanations suggest that poverty is not just a lack of money and may be caused or perpetuated by the poor themselves. These cultural explanations are often associated with the political right.

Later explanations concentrate on structural causes and emphasize inequality as a major cause of poverty. These explanations are favoured by the political left.

The dissolute poor

Poverty has been seen as the deserved result of weakness or wickedness. The tabloid press still tell us about 'scroungers' who neither need nor deserve benefits. Those in rich countries often perceive Third World poverty in these terms.

The unfortunate poor

After the Second World War it was widely thought that the problem of poverty was disappearing because of:

▶ the expansion of the Welfare State;
▶ economic growth brought higher wages; and
▶ there was full employment.

The few who were still recognized as poor were seen as special individual cases such as the old, the sick or the disabled.

The culture of poverty

This suggests that poverty is not just a lack of money but also that the poor are different from the rest of society. There are different views on the relationship between this culture and living in poverty. The alternatives include:

1 (An inferior) *culture* causes *poverty*.
2 *Poverty* causes (an inferior) *culture* which maintains *poverty* (O. Lewis).
3 *Poverty* causes (a positive adaptive) *culture* which helps the poor survive (C. and B. Valentine).

This third viewpoint does not blame poverty on the poor. Neither does Gans' view, namely that the culture of the non-poor encourages inequality that helps to maintain poverty.

Situational constraints
Critics of the cultural explanations claim that economic conditions limit the opportunities of the poor. Low pay, high unemployment and racial disadvantage all prevent the poor improving their position.

The failure of the Welfare State
The Welfare State has failed to prevent poverty and/or redistribute incomes.
  The *left* see benefits as inadequate to prevent poverty.
  The *new right* sociologists claim that poverty is perpetuated by making the poor dependent on benefits.

Weberian influenced accounts: the powerlessness of the poor
The poor may be weak not just because of their lack of money but also because they lack the power that comes through organizations such as political parties, pressure groups or trade unions.
  Vulnerable groups may include the old, the young, women, the sick and people with disabilities. Rex applied this Weberian analysis to ethnic minorities and immigrants.

Marxist influenced accounts
Poverty is seen as the inevitable result of inequality resulting from the exploitation of the working class in capitalist societies.

Women and poverty
Feminists have argued that women are particularly vulnerable to poverty.
  Women are seen as a distinctive group in the labour market(s). They often work part-time and tend to do 'women's jobs' which are often low paid. Marriage and motherhood may make women dependent on men or, in many cases, on the State.

The new right
Murray suggested that the poor, largely found in inner-city ghettoes, are to blame for their poverty and that they are poor by choice. The culture of poverty is passed on to children.
  British versions from politicians, the media or sociologists, tend to emphasize ethnicity less but share the views on the adverse effects of welfare dependence.

REVISION ACTIVITY

Identify the characteristics of each theory of poverty in the table below. Place a tick in the appropriate box.

The different theories of poverty

Theory	Left wing	Right wing	Blames the individual	Blames the poor	Structural	Cultural	Blames the Welfare State
Spencer							
Culture of poverty (Lewis)							
Culture of poverty (Valentine)							
Marxist							
Weberian (Townsend)							
Weberian (Rex)							
New right (Marsland)							
New right (Murray)							
Feminist							

EXAMINATION QUESTIONS

Question 1
(a) Briefly explain what is meant by a culture of poverty. *(4 marks)*
(b) Outline *two* problems faced by sociologists in attempting to measure the extent of poverty in contemporary society. *(4 marks)*
(c) 'Most people living in poverty are women.' Explain this statement. *(7 marks)*
(d) Critically assess the view that policies designed to eliminate poverty only cause increased dependency. *(10 marks)*

Total: 25 marks
(IBS, 1996)

Question 2
'Some have argued that the major reasons for the continuation of poverty are the behaviour and attitudes of the poor.' Critically discuss the sociological arguments and evidence in support of this view. *(25 marks)*

(AEB, 1996)

Question 3
Assess the argument that different definitions and explanations of poverty reflect different ideologies. *(25 marks)*

(AEB, 1995)

6 Power and politics

Many of the sources used in the study of power and politics do not come from mainstream sociology. This means you must learn to use theories borrowed from the various schools of political science rather than merely apply the major sociological perspectives.

When studying *the nature and distribution of power and the role of the State*, you could, for example, use:

▶ Marxist approaches.

And criticize with:

▶ Pluralist approaches; and
▶ Elite theories.

These theories are rarely used outside this A-level topic. They are usually more applicable to power and politics questions than more general sociological theories such as functionalism, interactionism or feminism.

Similarly, the popular voting-behaviour questions often require reference to specific theories which address this issue rather than a more general application of major sociological perspectives.

However, a good *sociological* answer will include a sound analysis of the importance of mainstream sociological concepts, such as class.

Political science may dominate the discussion of more visible political institutions such as:

▶ the State;
▶ government;
▶ political parties; and
▶ pressure groups,

but sociology has become increasingly interested in

▶ new social movements

and remains interested in

▶ mass media.

Key words and their definitions

Power   the ability to achieve your will against the will of others.

Authority   legitimate power.

Ideology   a set of ideas, based on values, which serve particular interests.

Hegemony   domination based on the consent of those who accept the ideology of the powerful.

The ruling class   a Marxist term describing those who have political power because they own the means of production.

Elites   groups whose power or influence is based on factors other than ownership. The concept, though usually found in conflict theories, is used to criticize Marxists.

Parties   organizations who seek to govern to achieve their common aims.

Pressure groups   organizations who seek to influence government decisions but not actually govern.

The State   a political apparatus that rules over a particular territory, which has legal authority and the ability to use force.

TOPIC OUTLINE

1 The nature and distribution of power

You will need to be able to describe the approaches of:

▶ **Marxists:**   Power is concentrated in the hands of the ruling class and is based on ownership.

▶ **Weberians:**   Power is distinguished from authority. The sources of legitimacy are examined.

▶ **Functionalists:** have a variable-sum view of power. (All the other approaches have a fixed-sum view.) Power is used to achieve consensual goals.

▶ **Pluralists:**   Power is widely dispersed between competing groups. Power is examined by studying decision-making.

▶ **Elite theorists:** Power will always be concentrated in the hands of an elite who will use it to promote their minority interests. The power of elites may be based on non-economic resources, such as organizational skills.

2 The role of the State

You will need to be able to describe the approaches of:

▶ **Marxists:**   the State is seen as part of the *superstructure* of *capitalist society*.

▶ **Weberians:**   the State is seen as an increasingly important *bureaucratic organization* with power that is not dependent on economic factors.

▶ **Functionalists:** the State is potentially an *integrating* force which can facilitate *goal attainment*.

▶ **Pluralists:**   the State as 'honest broker'.

▶ **New right:**   who argue for a *minimalist State*.

3 The ruling class

The dispute over the existence of a ruling class is largely conducted as a debate between:

Marxists versus **pluralists** and **elite theorists**

Writers such as C.W. Mills borrow from both Marx and Weber.

4 Political participation

This involves:

▶ **voting;**

▶ **membership of parties or pressure groups;**

- **holding office**;
- **decision-making**;
- **direct action**; and
- **violence**.

Participants tend to come from more advantaged groups who feel they are 'insiders' in society. This usually means white, middle-aged, higher class males.

There are organizations that are exceptions to this rule, such as women's groups, organizations for ethnic minorities and trade unions.

Theories of voting behaviour

The major sociological issue explored in questions about voting behaviour is the extent to which social class influences voting.

Sociological explanations of voting behaviour suggest various relationships between social class and voting:

1 Traditional theories see *class as the major correlate* with voting and suggest that *political socialization* explains the voters choice.
2 Theories of *deviant voting* were necessary to explain the defeat of working-class parties such as the Labour Party while there was a majority of manual workers in the electorate.

   Explanations given for deviant voting were as follows:
   (a) The *embourgeoisement* of the working class.
   (b) *Deferential working-class voters* who saw Conservative leaders as their social superiors.
   (c) *Instrumental voters* who calculated their individual interests and were not loyal to parties.
   (d) The existence of '*middle-class radicals*' who voted Labour. These tended to be better educated, in the caring professions and often employed in the public sector.
   (e) *Social mobility* may have meant that voters stayed loyal to the party of their youth rather than that associated with their new social position.
3 Theories that argue for:
   - class dealignment and
   - partisan dealignment

   and thus the unravelling of the relationship between class and support for political parties. Party image here becomes increasingly important.

   The reasons suggested for class dealignment are:
   (a) Changes in the occupational structure which led to the shrinking of the traditional working class who remain loyal to Labour. Crewe distinguished:
   - The Old Working Class of public sector workers, council house dwellers living in the North and Scotland (perhaps he should have added Wales)
   - The New Working Class who work in the private sector, are owner occupiers and live in the South.
   (b) The middle classes have also become divided. Routine clerical workers, particularly those in unions and working in the public sector, are less loyal to the Conservatives. Many of these are women.
   (c) All classes have become increasingly affluent. The ownership of homes and shares and optimism about the economic future are often associated with voting Conservative.
4 Theories that identify *other social characteristics* which influence choice, including:
   - *cultural divisions* such as nationality, language, religion and ethnicity, for example, Scottish and Welsh nationalism;
   - *geographical divisions* based on region or housing in urban, suburban or rural areas, for example, the North–South divide in Britain; and
   - *age, generation and gender.*
5 *Rational choice* theories that see the voter as an informed *consumer* who weighs up

issues, policies and images of parties and leaders.

6 Radical views that see the continuing importance of class and identify a *sectoral cleavage* between those who are involved as both consumer and worker in the private sector of the economy and those who are involved primarily in the public sector. The concept of ideology (also found in Parkin's view on deviant voters) is important in explaining voting behaviour.

7 The *return to social class* explanations that argue for an updated view of the class structure which allows prediction of voting. Heath suggests five classes.

This replaces the traditional simplistic division between a single working class of manual workers and a middle class of non-manual workers. Heath believes that short-term political factors are also important.

You will have noticed the absence of feminist perspectives. These can be introduced as follows:

Feminist theories of the State

▶ The Welfare State, employment law and policy and the criminal justice system have all reinforced women's traditional subservient family roles.

▶ Even in 'democratic' societies, women have been excluded from political activity because it is seen as a *public* activity whereas women have been confined to the *private* life of the home.

Feminist explanations of women's participation in the political process

▶ Conventional politics seem to be primarily concerned with male issues. This is seen as 'normal' and gender politics are seen as a marginal concern.

▶ Feminists have challenged the stereotypical view that women are not interested in politics and/or they are 'naturally' conservative and probably Conservative Party supporters.

Feminist views on patriarchy and patriarchal ideology: the struggle between patriarchy and feminism

▶ Patriarchy is the exercise of power by men over women.

▶ Patriarchal ideology is the set of ideas which legitimizes this domination.

▶ Men's resistance to votes for women should be considered, as well as women's struggle for emancipation.

▶ Women's movements have made personal issues, such as sexuality, into political issues.

REVISION ACTIVITY

Place the appropriate choice in each column in the table on page 45.

1 **Perspective**
   (a) Conflict
   (b) Consensus

2 **Source of power**
   (a) Ownership of the means of production
   (b) Derived from authority. Rulers rule with consent
   (c) Various; includes organizational skill, psychological factors, military, political or economic resources

3 **Who holds power?**
   (a) Concentrated in the hands of an exclusive minority?
   (b) Concentrated in the hands of a ruling class
   (c) Dispersed between competing groups

4 **How do new rulers emerge?**
   (a) Revolutionary change in the infrastructure. Changes in the governing group through election or coup is not a real change

(b) Ruling group 'loses vigour'. Changing social, not just economic, circumstances

(c) Elections to leading positions

5 The role of the State

(a) Neutral arbiter of competing interests

(b) Instrument of minority power

(c) Part of the superstructure of exploitative societies. Will wither away in a classless society

Sociological theory	Marxist	Elite theory	Pluralist
Perspective			
Source of power			
Who holds power?			
How do new rulers emerge?			
The role of the State			

EXAMINATION QUESTIONS

Question 1

(a) Briefly outline what sociologists mean by the State. *(4 marks)*

(b) Using examples of each, briefly distinguish between parties and pressure groups. *(4 marks)*

(c) Outline the elitist theory of power. *(7 marks)*

(d) Assess the strengths and weaknesses of the pluralist theory of power. *(10 marks)*

(IBS, 1995)

Question 2

Compare and contrast Marxist and new right perspectives on the role of the State in society. *(25 marks)*

(AEB, 1996)

Question 3

To what extent has the concept of the 'deviant voter' been relevant and useful in sociological accounts of voting behaviour? *(25 marks)*

(AEB, 1995)

7 Religion

Do not just commit the most important theories to memory, waiting for the chance to regurgitate them at the first mention of religion. Try to develop an *understanding* of the various theories and studies that can be used to answer a variety of questions.

The major theories of religion were developed during the early days of modern capitalist societies. In order to *apply* these to contemporary societies, you need to *assess* whether they still help us to understand the role of religion in society today.

Spend some time thinking about recent events to see if they support the role of religion as explained by Marx, Durkheim or Weber. A good argument with fellow students might help you to explore some of the more controversial and more interesting events. For example:

▶ What evidence is there for the rise of Christian, Hindu, Islamic, Jewish or Sikh fundamentalism?
▶ Does the rise of fundamentalism challenge the secularization thesis?
▶ Is fundamentalism necessarily conservative or can it be a force for change?
▶ Does the rise of fundamentalism support or refute the claims of Marxism, functionalism or Weberian approaches?

This kind of discussion will gain *interpretation* and *application* marks.

Key words and their definitions

Religion   there is no agreed definition but sociologists are concerned with these three aspects of religion: belief, behaviour, institutions.

Secularization   involves the decline in the influence of religion on the wider society and the reduction in the spiritual content of religious belief.

New religious movements   a collective term for religious groups which have recently emerged in Western societies. These may not be Christian.

Sects   according to Wilson, these are 'Exclusive bodies which impose some test of merit … faith, knowledge or obedience.' Often seen as having broken away from Christian churches.

Cults   arguably, religious groups whose beliefs and practices are more concerned with this world than more spiritual matters.

Social change   developments in the basic structures of a society, such as the economy, the political system or the family. These may be accompanied by cultural changes, for example, from traditional to modern society to postmodern society.

Social solidarity   the feelings of belonging and mutual interest which integrate the individual into society.

Fundamentalism   either *conservative fundamentalism*, which asserts traditional religious and social values, or *radical fundamentalism*, which rejects corrupt forms of religion and society and wishes to return to original roots.

TOPIC OUTLINE

1 The classical theories

You need to be able to *explain* and *evaluate* the main assumptions of Marxist, functionalist and Weberian theories of the role of religion in society.

Marx
► Religious beliefs and institutions are part of the superstructure of exploitative (pre-Communist) societies.
► Religion helps to reproduce the existing relations of production. It legitimizes inequality.
► Religion inhibits social change.
► Religious belief is ideological. It encourages a false consciousness for the working class since suffering, deprivation and poverty are seen as divinely ordered.
► Religion is a form of social control.

Functionalism
► Society is seen as a system of inter-related parts.
► The system has needs which must be met if it is to survive and remain stable. The functional needs satisfied by religion are:
  1 *Integration*: shared beliefs, rituals and sacred objects provide a basis for social order based on consensual values. Durkheim saw religion as the worship of the moral order which makes up society.
  2 *Social control* (pattern maintenance): religion provides divine backing for important rules and the certainty of justice in the next world.

Weber
► Rejects economic determinism.
► Sees ideas as influencing social structure.
► Associates the rise of capitalism with Protestantism.
► Sees religion as potentially a force for social change.
► Predicts the disenchantment of modern society which is seen as increasingly rational.

2 Other theories

Berger and Luckman – an interactionist view of religion

► Every society has a body of knowledge by which it makes sense of the world. This 'universe of meaning' must be constantly justified and reinforced.
► Berger and Luckman see the 'universe of meaning' as a *social construction*, not just an individual making sense of the world.
► Religion puts mankind in a central position in the whole universe.

Feminist perspectives on religion
► Religious beliefs can be seen as patriarchal ideology.
► Both religious institutions and beliefs help to legitimize gender inequality.
► Religion frequently supports the ideology of family life. The family is the location for the social control of women and children.
► Religious beliefs may legitimize male ownership, the inheritance of property and the division of labour based on gender.
► Obedience to husbands may be legitimized by religion.

3 The secularization debate

Identify the views of the classical theories as to secularization. All three predict a degree of secularization in modern societies.

Explain the different definitions of secularization. You may find it useful to focus on three different aspects of religion:

▶ religious behaviour;
▶ religious institutions; and
▶ religious belief.

Be able to assess the extent to which contemporary societies have become secularized.

Secularization: some additional concepts

▶ *Desacralization* is the loss of the ability to experience a sense of the sacred or mystery in life, and ceasing to believe that supernatural forces control the world.

Weber refers to this as *disenchantment* following the rise of scientific and rational thinking. This refers to what is going on in the mind of the individual and group, whereas secularization refers to the declining impact of religion on society.

▶ *Disengagement* is the separation of church from everyday society.
▶ *Structural differentiation* is the specialization of social organizations such as the church or family and is, according to Parsons, a feature of modern society. For example, churches have abandoned some of their education and welfare functions to focus on specifically religious matters.
▶ *Individuation*: according to Bellah, members of modern society are not materialistic, rational and secular. They are religious as individuals, not as church members. Critics of Bellah say his definition of religion as a search for meaning in life is itself a widening of the definition of religion to such an extent that it is evidence of secularization.

4 New religious movements (NRMs)

▶ Be able to assess the different explanations of the origin and development of sects and other NRMs such as:
   – alienation;
   – anomie;
   – rationalization and materialism; and
   – deprivation (economic, social, psychic).
▶ Use the growth of NRMs to support arguments for and against secularization.
▶ More traditional questions may ask you to define and distinguish different kinds of religious institutions, such as church, denomination, sect and cult, and also different types of sects, such as world-affirming, world-accommodating and world-rejecting. This may help with your discussion of the success of NRMs.

REVISION ACTIVITY

One of the major reasons for the persistence of the secularization debate is the disagreement between sociologists over the meaning of certain events and trends.

Complete the table indicating how a particular piece of evidence has been interpreted differently by sociologists. Where possible you may wish to name sociologists associated with an argument.

Evidence	Assessment	
	For secularization	Against secularization
Decline in church attendance	Religious behaviour is in decline	Attendance is not essential for some religions. Observation has become an individual matter.
Decline in other forms of participation, such as dietary rules, rites of passage		
Disengagement of Church from State		
Growing acceptance of scientific/rational thinking		
Decline in traditional moral behaviour, such as acceptance of divorce, abortion and homosexuality		
Growth of new religious movements		

EXAMINATION QUESTIONS

Question 1

'The main function of religion in society is the control of weaker social groups by the more powerful.' Evaluate sociological arguments both for and against this statement. *(25 marks)*

(AEB, 1996)

Question 2

(a) Identify *two* features of secularization. *(4 marks)*
(b) Identify and illustrate *two* criticisms of the secularization thesis. *(4 marks)*
(c) Outline the evidence for the secularization of the UK. *(7 marks)*
(d) Examine the reasons for the changes in institutional religion in the UK. *(10 marks)*

(IBS, 1996)

Question 3

Critically examine the sociological contributions to an understanding of the relationship between religion and social change in society. *(25 marks)*

(AEB, 1994)

8 Deviance, crime and social control

Deviance is one of the most popular topics to study, favoured by both students and teachers. Deviance, and particularly crime, is also a topic which is subject to considerable interest in the media and in the political arena. Thus there seems to be a continual increase in the amount of research published and in the offering of new explanations and solutions to the problem of crime.

There are a number of revision strategies you can adopt to help you reduce the knowledge you must learn and to maximize its value across this and other topics:

▶ Learn three or four major approaches and regard other theories as developments of these.
▶ Make the links between the old and the new. This should make it easy to understand and learn. What appears to be new sociology is often a development of older material rather than entirely new, for example, the Marxist and interactionist influences in the New Criminology.
▶ Learn criticisms of theories and studies rather than details of research.
▶ Apply older theories to the present. For example, Miller's sub-cultural theory can be applied to contemporary football hooliganism.
▶ Use your knowledge of theory and methods, such as the arguments about the positivist use of official statistics.
▶ Use your knowledge of deviance to illustrate theory and methods questions, for example, to help explain interactionist theory.

Key words and their definitions

Anomie   the loss of moral regulation in society. Social norms no longer restrain individual behaviour.

Deviance   behaviour which breaks society's rules. Most sociologists agree that deviance is socially defined and is not an intrinsic quality of particular kinds of behaviour.

Deviants   the definition of a deviant depends on the view of the sociologist. Deviants are people who have broken the rules and/or been labelled as rulebreakers.

Crime   behaviour which breaks the law, which is rules made by the State.

White-collar crime   crime committed by the middle classes in their work places, for example, embezzling funds.

Social order   the predictable nature of social life. It may be based on consensual values or imposed by the powerful.

Social control   the process of enforcing the norms of society. It helps to ensure social order.

Labelling theory   suggests that people become deviant after they have been labelled as rulebreakers by the police, the courts and others. It is associated with the interactionist perspective.

The positivist approach suggests that deviance, ill health, etc. can have social rather than individual causes. Conflict theorists use positivist studies to attribute 'blame' for deviance/ill health to socially structured inequalities and pressures rather than to individual misdeeds or misfortune.

TOPIC OUTLINE

1 The evaluation of major theories

You should be able to develop further and criticize the major characteristics of these explanations.

Durkheimian explanations

- ▶ consensus perspective;
- ▶ structuralist perspective;
- ▶ positivist approach often using crime statistics;
- ▶ deviance defined as rulebreaking;
- ▶ deviants seen as different from 'normal people';
- ▶ social control based on agreed rules.

Marxist explanations

- ▶ conflict perspective;
- ▶ structuralist perspective;
- ▶ positivist approach but suspicious of official statistics;
- ▶ deviance defined by ruling class;
- ▶ deviance is normal in capitalist society for both classes;
- ▶ social control imposed on working class.

Interactionist explanations

- ▶ conflict perspective;
- ▶ individualist perspective;
- ▶ interpretive approach sees crime statistics as a social construction;
- ▶ deviance defined as being successfully labelled;
- ▶ primary deviance seen as normal. People may be labelled because they are different;
- ▶ social control creates and amplifies deviance.

Feminist approaches

- ▶ conflict perspective;
- ▶ structuralist perspective;
- ▶ rejects positivist methods (usually). Crime statistics seen as unreliable;
- ▶ deviance defined by patriarchal ideology;
- ▶ some offences against women are seen as normal in patriarchal society;
- ▶ social control imposed on women reduces the number of offences.

You could usefully expand on each of the approaches outlined above and note any criticisms. You might also consider studies which throw light on each approach. The box on page 53 gives an example of how you might do this in the case of the 'Interactionist Explanations'.

Example Interactionist explanations
Further development
The shared perspective is individualistic rather than structuralist. Some writers acknowledge the influence of power in the creation of social order. The major theoretical influences are symbolic interactionism and ethnomethodology. The dominant approach is anti-positivist. It is this that unifies these various studies.

A deviant is seen not as a rulebreaker but as someone who has been processed as a deviant, i.e. successfully labelled deviant. The main question is 'Why are some people more likely to be so labelled?'

The methods associated with this approach try to describe the interaction or negotiation between 'offenders' and various forms of social institutions and agencies such as the police, the courts and the media. Crime statistics are seen not as a useful resource, but as a subject to study. It is suggested that they describe police and judicial procedures, rather than the criminals.

The role of the media in amplifying deviance and causing moral panics can be an examination question in its own right. Minor non-criminal deviance, or even non-offenders, are studied as well as criminal deviance. Studies include mental illness, stuttering and the innocent.

Critics
Positivists claim that interactionists avoid the most important issue, which is explaining crime.

Marxists share the view of differential law enforcement and the problematic nature of crime, but criticize interactionists for not considering the influence of structural inequality on justice.

Studies
▶ Becker asks why some people, and acts, are labelled deviant. He sees the consequences of the acts as important in this labelling process, rather than the acts themselves. In other words, social reaction to the acts and the characteristics of offenders and victims are important factors. He also asks 'Who makes the rules?'
▶ Cicourel provides, perhaps, the best interactionist critique of crime statistics. He also introduces the ethnomethodologists' concept of commonsense assumptions to explain the behaviour of law enforcers.
▶ Lemert emphasizes the importance of social reaction in transforming primary deviance to secondary deviance.
▶ J. Young gives an interactionist account of the role of the police in the amplification of deviance. He provides a useful account of crime waves, which can be used to criticize crime statistics. In his more recent work, which has been described as 'left realist', he measures crime in a more positivist way through victim studies.

2 The evaluation of other theories

The new criminology
▶ combines the insights of interactionist and Marxist theories;
▶ explains the interaction between 'offenders' and police by looking at the difference in power found in capitalist society;
▶ sees some deviance as political resistance to the ruling class;
▶ used to explain higher apparent crime rates among ethnic minorities.

New left realism

▶ reaction against new criminology;
▶ crime seen as a real problem for the working class;
▶ considers victims as well as offenders;
▶ structural causes of crime are **marginalization**, **relative deprivation** and **subculture**.

New right theories

▶ emphasize cultural rather than structural causes;
▶ reject the view that capitalism causes crime;
▶ associate crime with the underclass.

The social distribution of deviance

Questions may ask you to explain the different rates of deviance, and in particular recorded crime, for different social groups. You should select from the explanations above to explain the different rates by:

▶ **age**
▶ **class**
▶ **ethnicity**
▶ **gender**
▶ **locality**

If questions ask about 'involvement in crime', you can discuss the victims as well as the offenders.

The suicide debate

The sociology of suicide may be examined as a form of deviance or used to illustrate methodological debates.

The critical assessment of Durkheim's work allows us to discuss a variety of sociological issues. These include:

▶ explaining the social distribution of suicide;
▶ evaluating the functionalist explanation of suicide;
▶ explaining the social construction of suicide and suicide statistics;
▶ evaluating the positivist approach to sociology;
▶ assessing the usefulness of the comparative survey; and
▶ assessing the usefulness of secondary data, and official statistics in particular.

★ REVISION ACTIVITY

The table on page 55 is intended to compare functionalist and interactionist approaches to deviance. Place the appropriate letter or letters in the correct box.

1 (a) conflict
   (b) consensus

2 (a) positivist
   (b) interpretive

3 (a) breaking agreed rules
   (b) being processed as a deviant

4 (a) they create deviance by labelling 'offenders'
   (b) assumed to be neutral enforcers of consensual rules

5 (a) can be a useful resource to explain deviance
   (b) are a topic worth studying in their own right
   (c) are socially constructed by police and courts
   (d) are a more or less accurate record of crime

6 (a) falsely assumes a consensus of values
   (b) underestimates the importance of class inequality
   (c) does not explain primary deviance
   (d) neglects the study of women
   (e) fails to see that crime statistics are unrepresentative

	Functionalist	Interactionist
1 Perspective		
2 Research approach		
3 Definition of deviance		
4 Attitude to police and courts		
5 Attitude to crime statistics		
6 Major criticisms		

EXAMINATION QUESTIONS

Question 1
(a) Briefly outline what sociologists mean by a 'moral panic'. *(4 marks)*
(b) Briefly identify and illustrate *two* aspects of the relationship between ethnicity and crime in the UK. *(4 marks)*
(c) Outline the weaknesses suggested by sociologists in the police statistics on the relationship between ethnic groups and crime. *(7 marks)*
(d) Examine the claim that 'popular' views of black criminality are 'myths'. *(10 marks)*

(IBS, 1996)

Question 2
Examine critically the relationship between deviance and power. *(25 marks)*

(AEB, 1996)

Question 3
'Many sociological approaches to deviance have ignored the extent to which females are involved in crime.' Discuss the evidence and arguments for and against this view. *(25 marks)*

(AEB, 1995)

Theory and methods

SOLUTION TO REVISION ACTIVITY

More scientific	More Interpretive/Meaningful
Quantitative	Qualitative
Detached	Involved
Objective	Subjective
Reliable	Understanding
Representative	In-depth

3	5	1	7	4	6	2

If you do not agree with my judgement, make sure you can argue your case. You may also wish to identify a study which uses each method.

ANSWERS TO EXAMINATION QUESTIONS

Question 1

'The purpose of the experiment is to create a standardized situation for the researcher to study, in which variables are under the control of the experimenter.' Evaluate the contribution experiments make to a sociological understanding of social behaviour. (IBS, 1996)

To achieve high marks for this question you need to demonstrate:

1 An understanding of the experimental method. You should explain both the logic (thinking) and the techniques (doing) associated with experimentation.

Mention the testing of hypotheses by manipulating an independent variable (cause) and observing the dependent variable (effect) while controlling extraneous variables (the 'standardized situation' mentioned in the question).

2 The case *for* the experiment. Mention:
  ▶ theoretical issues, such as the link with positivism and value freedom; and
  ▶ practical issues, such as control and reliability.

3 The case *against* the experiment. Mention:
  ▶ theoretical issues;
  ▶ practical issues; and
  ▶ ethical issues.

4 You could also discuss other sociological methods that use the logic of the experiment, but for practical reasons do not follow all the techniques, for example, Durkheim's advocating of the comparative survey as the best sociological substitute for the natural science experiment.

There is a (limited) range of sociological studies that have used the experimental method. Surprisingly, many of these do not follow a positivist approach.

You can use these to support the arguments made above or separately to evaluate the contribution made to the understanding of social behaviour. The first two examples have implications for sociological and perhaps natural science research in general. The last two are from an interpretive point of view which challenges positivism.

- The Hawthorne studies included an experiment to test the effect of lighting on production. The studies revealed the 'experimenter effect' where merely taking part in research changes the behaviour of subjects.
- Rosenthal and Jacobson showed that the self-fulfilling prophecy influenced the behaviour of school pupils.
- Daniel used (field) experiments to test the extent of racial discrimination in employment, housing and the provision of services.
- Atkinson conducted an experiment where English and Danish coroners were presented with identical suicide casenotes and their verdicts were recorded. He used this research to challenge Durkheim's reliance on official statistics.
- Garfinkel used experiments to show that everyday behaviour is influenced by 'commonsense assumptions'. He created a situation where taken-for-granted rules were broken in order to reveal how subjects made sense of these novel situations.

Question 2 Student answers with examiner comments

Evaluate the ways in which scientific thinking and methods have influenced sociological research. (AEB, 1995)

> **Examiner's note**   All A-level questions require a specific response to the set question. This particular question is not an invitation to write a general account of science. It needs a balanced answer which evaluates the extent to which sociology has been influenced by the thinking and methods of science.
>   Better answers will discuss:
>
> 1 'Scientific thinking' for example, the hypodeductive approach and the commitment to objectivity.
> 2 The techniques used to gather and analyse data, for example, the more scientific methods favoured by positivists such as comparative surveys and the anti-scientific approach of much interactionist sociology.

Science can be defined as a body of verifiable knowledge collected by systematic research or the method by which such information is collected. Positivists believed that sociology could be a science by using scientific methods to get verifiable knowledge. Comte and Durkheim wanted to improve society by discovering the social laws that guided social behaviour. They believed that scientific thinking and methodology could be applied to the study of the social world.

> **Examiner's note**   Defines science, links it to positivism and explains why Comte and Durkheim favoured this approach.

Positivist sociologists argue that the hypodeductive method, which produces reliable, objective and verifiable data, can be used in sociological research. Therefore they prefer methods that produce quantitative data and allow correlations and causal laws to be established.

Positivists believe that scientific methodology can be used because they consider man to be part of the natural universe. Durkheim suggested that society was subject to social laws. Positivists believe in systematic, objective scientific methods of research. Positivists also believe that individuals react to external stimuli like other natural objects.

> **Examiner's note**   The case for the scientific approach is developed.

However, interactionists and other anti-positivists argue that humans do not respond to external stimuli and, unlike the natural world studied by scientists, have a consciousness. This means that actions are directed by motives and feelings. These anti-positivists believe that the study of social phenomena should be concerned with discovering the motives and meanings that guide behaviour (Weber's *verstehen*) rather than trying to establish causal relationships.

> **Examiner's note**   Evaluation from an interactionist perspective.

Positivists believe that sociology can be objective and value free, like the natural sciences. However, it is arguable whether science itself is objective. Kuhn suggested that the existence of scientific paradigms meant that scientists saw the physical world in a particular way rather than searching for the objective truth. Scientists also make value judgements about the subjects they study and they desire to prove their hypotheses correct. Popper overcame this problem by proposing the falsification method.

> **Examiner's note**   Discusses value freedom and the alleged objectivity of natural science.

Anti-positivists argue that sociology cannot be value free and objective. They argue that social phenomena are subjective and should be studied subjectively. Knowledge has a cultural base and researchers should use their knowledge to interpret and understand the actions of others. They argue that sociologists and scientists are guided by their own experience and culture. No research is neutral and objective. Sociologists may be Marxists, functionalists or feminists and this influences their research.

> **Examiner's note**   Positivism criticized and the ideological nature of some theories suggested.

Interactionists claim sociology cannot be objective and value free as the subject matter is different from the natural sciences and the sociologist should not be value free.
  Consequently, anti-positivists advocate the use of qualitative rather than quantitative methods such as participant observation. This produces more valid empathetic understanding (*verstehen*).

> **Examiner's note**   Introduces discussion of methods but little development.

A number of sociologists now advocate a mixed methodology or triangulation to produce reliable checkable data.

> **Examiner's note**   Lacks evaluative conclusion but raises new issues.

> **Examiner's comment**   Overall this is a sophisticated and well-developed answer. It does not deal at length with the techniques used by sociologists and their relationship to science. Nonetheless plenty of knowledge and above all understanding is shown here.
>   Interpretation and application are clear and convincing and there is an evaluative framework based on the critical discussion of positivism which is carried through the answer.

> Knowledge and understanding: *8 marks*
> Interpretation and application: *8 marks*
> Evaluation: *8 marks*
> Total: *24 marks*

> Clearly a Grade A. This shows that relatively brief answers can approach full marks.

Question 3

(a) Suggest *two* reasons why participant observation is a 'highly individual technique' (*Item A*, line 8). *(2 marks)*

One mark for each distinct reason such as:
- ▶ Normally undertaken by a lone researcher.
- ▶ You cannot generalize from the individual case.
- ▶ Depends on the individual skill of the researcher.
- ▶ The individual's research cannot be repeated by others.

(b) Identify *two* criticisms of 'letting the data speak for itself' in participant observation studies (*Item B*, line 11). *(2 marks)*

One mark for each distinct criticism, such as:
- ▶ Subjects may try to deceive the researcher.
- ▶ The researcher *still* selects and interprets data.
- ▶ Cannot generate testable hypotheses.
- ▶ Is subjective and non-scientific rather than objective and scientific.

(c) Suggest *two* problems that might be experienced by a researcher in undertaking covert participant observation. *(2 marks)*

One mark for each distinct problem, such as:
- ▶ gaining access to (secretive/exclusive) groups ;
- ▶ taking part in shameful/illegal activities;
- ▶ deceiving subjects is unethical;
- ▶ problems of recording data.

(d) With reference to *Item C* and elsewhere, assess the advantages and disadvantages of quantitative methods of social investigation. *(9 marks)*

A balanced assessment of both advantages and disadvantages is required. You should support your arguments by applying appropriate studies. You could discuss the following issues:
- ▶ objectivity;
- ▶ generalization/representativeness;
- ▶ testing hypotheses;
- ▶ control, reliability and validity;
- ▶ scientific methods;
- ▶ the case for methodological pluralism.

You can refer to studies using experiments and various kinds of surveys employing primary or secondary data.

(e) With references to the *Items* and other sources, evaluate the claim that in participant-observation studies, what is gained in terms of validity is lost in reliability. *(10 marks)*

The key factor in achieving a high grade is to explicitly address the concepts of reliability and validity. The question is asking for something more focused than a general critical review of participant observation.

Make sure for this and other questions that you can define, explain and illustrate the concepts of reliability and validity. A good answer might suggest that there may be a link between theoretical perspective and the researcher's attitude towards using participant observation. Interactionists may favour sacrificing objectivity for subjectivity and, in their view, validity.

2 The family

SOLUTION TO REVISION ACTIVITY

The symmetrical family: Evidence and arguments

For
1, 2, 3, 5, 8(?), 9, 11

Against
4, 6, 8(?), 10, 12

7 may be true but is not really relevant to the discussion.

8 It depends how much men 'help' and how much sociologists think they should. The symmetrical family does not mean that the roles of men and women are the same. But it does suggest that their roles have become more equal: men are seen as doing more around the house. Oakley, however, was dismissive that 'help' actually indicated that women's domestic labour burden had been significantly reduced. She argued that the family was still unequal.

11 is Parsons' view of the isolated modern nuclear family. You may feel that it could be used as an argument against the symmetrical family.

ANSWERS TO EXAMINATION QUESTIONS

Question1 Student answer with examiner comments

(a) Which sociological perspective is illustrated by *Item A*? *(1 mark)*

Marxist.

> **Examiner's note** 1/1 Sufficient for the mark.

(b) Explain briefly what is meant by 'patriarchal ideology'. (*Item B*, lines 1–2) *(2 marks)*

It is the ideology of male domination. A way of thinking or ideas which support male power.

> **Examiner's note** 2/2 1 mark each for explaining patriarchal and ideology.

(c) *Item C* states that 'in most societies, the two people who produce a child are expected to take responsibility for its upbringing' (lines 11–12). How far is this view supported by sociological evidence? *(5 marks)*

This view is supported by functionalists who see the nuclear family as usually the most efficient agent for the upbringing of children. Indeed, in modern Britain many of the responsibilities associated with raising a child are regarded as those of the parents. This continues to apply even when parents are divorced and they continue to care for and pay for children.

There are alternatives to these practices. Extended family members may take or share responsibility for childcare. In some simple societies, child-raising is a group activity.

> ***Examiner's note*** Good evaluative stance.
> Examples and/or research evidence would help. Perhaps refer to research on working-class or Asian families in Britain.

We must also consider systems of child-raising such as adoption, fostering and children's homes. Here the two people who bear the child are not mainly responsible for it. Instead responsibility may be shared between the State and the carers, or be with adoptive parents.

Thus although natural parents usually take responsibility, there are alternatives.

> ***Examiner's note*** 4/5 Relevant, accurate and evaluative. Lacks references to a range of sociological evidence.

(d) Assess the contribution of feminist perspectives to an understanding of the family. *(8 marks)*

Feminist perspectives have contributed to an understanding of the family by identifying housework as real productive work in the form of unpaid domestic labour. This is a major contribution to our understanding of the family, as housework is an integral part of the family situation. The housewife role has low status, is unpaid and dominates women's other roles. Feminism has thus enlightened our view of the housewife.

> ***Examiner's note*** Relevant application of knowledge of housework.

Feminists have suggested that marriage is a key factor in limiting the potential of women. This is true to some degree – men benefit the most from marriage according to Bernard, whereas women become worse off, physically and emotionally. Thus we are shown conjugal and family roles in a new light: rather than the symmetrical family, we are shown the significance of power in family relationships.

> ***Examiner's note*** Good application and finishes with an evaluative comment.

Feminism has also examined education as a means of understanding the family. The curriculum can often be gender-based and thus affect a girl's self-image. This may undermine confidence and the female attitude to work; women are concentrated in jobs that are extensions of the housewife–mother role.

> ***Examiner's note*** Unpredictable but sound application of education and work evidence.

However, to criticize feminist perspectives it is argued that women enjoy their roles and gain fulfilment from them. It is also said that because housework is fairly autonomous, it is better than supervised employment.

Feminist writers have also been said to lack objectivity and offer views which are too ideological. However, in my view, this could also be said to apply to non-feminist writers on the family, such as Parsons.

Thus feminist perspectives have contributed greatly to our understanding of the family by offering a valid alternative to the traditional views, such as those offered by Parsons.

> ***Examiner's note*** 6/8 Balanced and convincing arguments. Could be improved by considering a range of feminist perspectives.

(e) *Items A and C* suggest very different views about the functions of the family in modern society. Discuss these points of view and assess their relative merits. *(9 marks)*

Item A presents a Marxist view of the family based on a conflict view of society. The family is generally viewed negatively as part of the superstructure, reproducing the class structure. It is a means by which the ruling class can exert and maintain their dominance. Marxist theory says that the family serves the needs of the ruling class by maintaining and reproducing the existing relations of production in a variety of ways. Thus families are a way of preserving the exploitative relationship between the classes.

On the other hand, *Item C* shows that functionalist ideas on the family follow a consensus perspective. The family is seen as 'fitting the needs of society' and is the most important agent of socialization. Thus the family is viewed in a positive light.

Both views can be assessed for their merits and faults. Marxism, like feminism, recognizes that housework is unpaid but real productive work. The view of women as a reserve army of labour is useful to an extent in examining the relationship between the family and the wider society. However, it could also be said that Marxists start from an ideological position that condemns the family as an agency supporting capitalist values. They also fail to explain the similarities in the structure of the family between capitalist and non-capitalist societies.

Functionalism has positivist features, such as its emphasis on the role of the family in shaping the personality of the child. However, this view presents a conservative stance and suggests that the nuclear family must be the best possible organization. There is a sense of committed defence of the family in functionalist writing.

Examiner's note Functionalists are not uncritical of the nuclear family: they also offer functionalist explanations for the persistence of the extended family.

A valid alternative to both these views is the feminist perspective which is more consistent with the Marxist view than the traditional view of functionalists. Interactionists criticize the emphasis on structuralist explanations found in both Marxist and functionalist writing.

Examiner's note 7/9 Concludes with evaluation. A balanced answer in terms of criticism but demonstrates a better understanding of Marxism than functionalism.

20/25 Overall, clearly an A grade answer. This candidate is more comfortable with applying theory than with demonstrating knowledge of studies. She could improve her use of knowledge from the Items.

Question 2

(a) Briefly explain what sociologists mean by the concept of the 'isolated nuclear family'. *(4 marks)*

Your explanation must cover both parts of the concept: 'isolated' from extended family, neighbours and other social networks; 'nuclear' consisting of parents and children and not others.

(b) Identify two aspects of modern social life which are seen by some sociologists as promoting the spread of the isolated nuclear family. *(4 marks)*

You must identify an appropriate feature of modern social life and show how it affects the family. For example, the rehousing of families from traditional working-class communities in inner cities may break up ties between generations (Willmott and Young).

Increased social mobility weakens ties with extended family and past friends and neighbours.

Or: give reasonable alternatives referring to geographical mobility or the expansion of education.

(c) What evidence is there for the view that extended kinship remains significant in the UK? *(7 marks)*

You should apply a range of older and hopefully newer material to the set question. You could mention:
▶ ethnic minority and/or immigrant families;
▶ urban villages; and
▶ supportive networks within the working, middle and upper classes.
The distinction between family and household might be useful here, as might the significance of modern communications (such as air travel and telephones) which allow the maintenance of kinship networks over long distances.

(d) Evaluate the view that the isolation of the nuclear family contributes to marital instability and high divorce rates. *(10 marks)*

The emphasis must be on evaluation in your answer. You should assess both the strengths and weaknesses of the evidence and arguments that support and oppose this view.
     This is not just an invitation to criticize the nuclear family. You must consider the effects of 'isolation' on marital stability and divorce. The following evidence and arguments could be compared, contrasted and assessed:
▶ Marxism and feminism will offer alternative explanations of marital instability and rising divorce rates.
▶ 'Optimistic functionalists' would see rising divorce rates as the result of higher expectations of marriage, explaining instability at an individual level rather than in the family as an institution.
▶ The 'dark side' of the nuclear family was pointed out by Leach and Laing.

Question 3
(a) What do sociologists mean by 'functional prerequisites' (*Item A*, line 5) and 'cultural capital' (*Item C*, line 4)? *(10 marks)*

Functional prerequisites are the needs of the social system which must be met if the system is to survive and remain stable.
     Cultural capital is the set of valued skills, knowledge and attitudes which middle-class parents can pass on to their children.
     Or: other reasonable definitions.

(b) Suggest two sociological reasons why Dr Kiernan's results are seen as surprising. *(2 marks)*

Functionalist accounts of the family have stressed the importance of two parents.
     Divorce and single parenthood are perceived as social problems, for example, by new right writers.
     Or: other acceptable reasons.

(c) Assess the contribution of the functionalist approach identified in *Item A* to an understanding of the modern industrial family *(8 marks)*

A balanced answer is required to achieve high marks. The strengths and weaknesses of the functionalist approach must be assessed and the evidence cited focused on the set question: an understanding of the modern industrial family must be shown, not the family in general.
     Don't try to write everything you know about the family. Take note what is required in question 3(d) to avoid duplication.
1 You can organize your answer using different perspectives: using **Marxism**, **feminism** and perhaps **interactionism** and the **new right** as critical alternatives to functionalism.

2 Or you could consider the functionalist approach applied to:
- ▶ the **structure** of the modern family: how the isolated nuclear family fits the needs of industrial society; Marxist and historical criticism
- ▶ the **roles** within the modern family: discuss Parsons' view and the existence of the symmetrical family; refer to the sociology of childhood and feminist critiques of equality
- ▶ the **functions** of the family: discuss the alleged loss of functions and perhaps family disorganization.

(d) How far do you agree with the argument in *Item C* (lines 1–2) that 'the family has sustained class inequalities and patterns of exploitation'? *(6 marks)*

This is asking for a critical discussion of the Marxist view of the family as an institution which reproduces the existing relations of production.

There is lots of evidence and argument in *Item C* to help with the Marxist side of the argument.

Feminist views on the 'patterns of exploitation' can be offered as a critical alternative and you can apply the functionalist arguments in *Item A* to good effect.

Similarities, as well as differences, between perspectives can be used in evaluation.

(e) What have sociologists identified as the 'taken-for-granted assumptions about the natures of women and men' (*Item C,* lines 10–11) and how have these assumptions been criticized ? *(7 marks)*

The phrase 'taken-for-granted assumptions about the natures of women and men' suggests that gender roles are seen as natural and not questioned.

You should identify some of the characteristics of masculinity and femininity in contemporary society. You could then cite evidence to show that roles are socially constructed and, as such, are culturally and historically specific: they vary from time to time and place to place.

Your major source of criticism of the assumptions are likely to be feminist arguments and studies, although most sociological perspectives would challenge the 'naturalness' of roles.

3 Education

Identify *three* similarities and *three* differences between Marxist and functionalist explanations of the role of education in society.

(Any three similarities or differences from this list or any reasonable alternatives will gain the marks.)

1 Both study education by looking at its relationship with the wider society. Both are structuralist theories.
   ▶ Functionalism is a consensus theory, whereas Marxism is a conflict theory.
   ▶ Marxists see education as part of the superstructure of capitalist society shaped by the economic infrastructure and helping to reproduce the existing relations of production.
   ▶ Functionalists see the education system as contributing towards the survival and stability of the social system by satisfying various functional needs, such as integration and adaptation.
2 Both link education with the economy.
   ▶ Marxism sees education as reproducing capitalism, whereas functionalists see it as fitting the needs of industrial society.
   ▶ Functionalists emphasize training and role allocation, whereas Marxists emphasize the production of de-skilled obedient workers.
3 Both identify a cultural reproduction role.
   ▶ Functionalists emphasize the integrative effects of transmitting consensual values.
   ▶ Marxists talk of ruling-class ideology and maintaining false consciousness.

Question 1

(a) Briefly explain what is meant by the concept of 'cultural capital'. *(4 marks)*

Your answer should refer to:
Ideas and skills which are highly valued by the **dominant culture** and are **transmitted** by middle-class **parents** to their **children** who gain an **advantage** in **school** which is translated into continued **economic** advantage.
   For similar questions it is worth noting that **Bordieu** also wrote about **social capital** and **economic capital**.

(b) Identify *two* examples of skills and knowledge outside the formal curriculum that may contribute to educational success. *(4 marks)*

One mark each for identifying up to two examples. One mark each for explaining how they may contribute to educational success. For example,
   ▶ Parents knowing which are 'good' schools. These schools may offer better facilities.
   ▶ Children using an elaborate code of language. The children's language is more highly valued by teachers who expect more of these pupils.

(c) Outline how material factors might explain class differences in educational attainment. *(7 marks)*

The material factors must be identified and then used to explain class differences in educational attainment. For example:
▶ Higher incomes (Bordieu's economic capital) can buy private education, books and computers for home study.
▶ Low income may lead to poor diet which inhibits learning at school. It may also limit children's cultural experiences which might otherwise encourage learning.
▶ Low income may encourage early school-leaving and the inability to enter FE and HE on a full-time basis. Higher incomes allow parents and spouses to support the full-time education of their families.
▶ Poor housing may lead to ill health and absence from school. The lack of quiet, warm and private surroundings may inhibit home study.
▶ other reasonable alternatives.

(d) Assess the relative importance of cultural and material factors in sociological explanations of educational attainment. *(10 marks)*

Two of these 10 marks are reserved for quality of language. The other 8 are for presenting a full and balanced evaluation of both cultural and material factors.

The evidence and arguments used might be influenced by Marxist, feminist, functionalist, interactionist or new right approaches. They might be illustrated by reference to social class, gender or ethnicity. Relevant studies that could be mentioned include those by Bordieu, Bernstein, Ball, Willis and Barrett.

Question 2
(a) What does Jones suggest is the way in which schools 'legitimate male violence' *(Item A)*? *(1 mark)*

By making it 'seem part of everyday life'.

(b) Identify *both* factors which *Item B* suggests contribute to upward social mobility. *(1 mark)*

1 Individual intelligence.
2 Going to a good school.

(c) The concept of the self-fulfilling prophecy described in *Item C* has been criticized by some sociologists. Identify *three* ways in which the concept might be criticized. *(3 marks)*

1 Students may resist the teacher's expectations and behave differently from the way they were expected.
2 Measuring pupils' attainment is problematic.
3 It cannot be proven that changes in a pupil's performance are solely or mainly the result of the teacher's expectations.

(d) Using information from the *Items* and elsewhere, evaluate sociological contributions to an understanding of the hidden curriculum, as it affects *female* pupils. *(10 marks)*

▶ Define and explain the hidden curriculum.
▶ Distinguish from the formal curriculum.
▶ Interpret and apply points from items, for example, in *Item A*, 'teacher's attitudes', allocation of teacher's time, 'attitudes and behaviour of the students', 'legitimizng male violence'. (You look at *Items B* and *C*)
▶ Use any other knowledge you have of the hidden curriculum, such as references to the organization of the school, the gendered hierarchy of

employees, sexist learning materials. Make sure they are applied to the experience of female pupils.
- ▶ Try to use feminist (and other) theoretical perspectives in your evaluation and knowledge of concepts such as patriarchal ideology.
- ▶ The changes in the experience of girls in school, perhaps influenced by sociological research, can be used in your evaluation.

(e) Assess the extent to which school factors, such as those identified in the *Items*, explain the differential educational achievement between *social classes*. *(10 marks)*

- ▶ Interpret and apply points from items, for example, in *Item C* 'teachers make judgements', 'labels … based on commonsense knowledge' and the explanation of how the self-fulfilling prophecy works.
- ▶ Use a suitable framework to plan and present your answer, for example, *in school factors*
  1 the education system
  2 the school
  3 teacher–pupil interaction
- ▶ References to out-of-school factors must be used to **assess** the significance of in-school factors, not just listed as an alternative. These out-of-school factors will influence the experience of the child in school.

Question 3 Student answer with examiner comments

(a) According to *Item C*, from which social groups did children who under-achieve come? *(1 mark)*

Children from semi-skilled or unskilled working-class homes.

(b) Evaluate sociological explanations of the 'poor school progress' made by some children from West Indian and Asian homes (*Item B*). *(8 marks)*

Eysenck found that Black children have lower IQ levels than White children. Most sociologists explain this difference as being the result of different environments not due to innate differences.

> ***Examiner's note*** Some evaluation of a psychological approach.

Coard believed that 'poor school progress' among ethnic minorities was a result of the education system. He found that the system treated them as inferior and inadequate. Consequently the children were labelled as inferior, saw themselves as being inferior, behaved in an inferior way and so did not achieve their potential because of this self-fulfilling prophecy.

> ***Examiner's note*** School-based explanations.
> Evaluated at end of answer.

The Swann Report also blamed poor progress on the school, not the child. It claimed that social inequalities and racial discrimination were the causes.

> ***Examiner's note*** More relevant evidence needed.

Ethnic minorities share similar problems and inequalities to working-class children.

> ***Examiner's note*** This is a weak attempt at a linking sentence which attempts to make class evidence on class relevant to a question about ethnicity. A better answer would make some attempt to apply this evidence to the set question, for example, by asking if cultural and linguistic differences might influence the performance of ethnic minorities.

Douglas saw that primary socialization in the home provides more stimulation for middle-class children. He also claimed that parental interest in education was lower in working-class families.

Bernstein believed that working-class children learned the restricted code of language at home whereas middle-class children also learned the elaborate code. The elaborate code is more valued in schools.

Bordieu has similar views. His theory talks of cultural capital which is reproduced in the education system and enables middle-class children to succeed.

Halsey claimed that material deprivation limits the opportunities of some children who lack stimulating toys.

Sugarman and Willis both claim that the subculture of the working class transmits values of fatalism, so children do not succeed.

> **Examiner's note** This final paragraph returns to the question. Sound evaluation with evidence of labelling theories.

Fuller found that some Black girls who had been labelled 'inferior' rebelled against their negative label and passed their exams. This suggests that the self-fulfilling prophecy theory does not always produce failure.

> **Examiner's note** 5/8 Misses opportunities to apply knowledge to set question. Evaluation rather limited.

(c) To what extent do you agree that teachers' judgements of pupils are the main cause of under-achievement in schools? Refer to the *Items* and other evidence in your answer. *(8 marks)*

Interactionists found that teachers' judgements of pupils can greatly influence the pupil's performance. Rosenthal and Jacobson told teachers that certain of their pupils would experience rapid intellectual growth. Later, when measured, these children had experienced intellectual growth. They concluded that the self-fulfilling prophecy was right and that teachers reveal their opinions of pupils through interaction in the classroom.

> **Examiner's note** This study is focused on the set question and is essentially accurate. If this study is to be used in a methods question it would be worth noting that the researchers randomly assigned pupils to experimental and control groups.

However, M. Fuller pointed out that the teachers' judgement can have a positive or a negative effect. She found that a group of Black girls had been predicted to fail but they reacted to the negative label by working hard to pass. So the effect of teachers' judgements is not always predictable.

> **Examiner's note** Fuller used again in a critical fashion. It might be worth explaining that gender and ethnicity influence judgements.

Hargreaves found that teachers go through three stages of classifying pupils. The first is speculation based on the appearance and conduct of the child. The second is elaboration, where the teacher finds evidence to support or refute her idea of the pupil. The final stage is stabilization where the teacher believes they know the pupil and is not surprised by their conduct. After the stabilization phase pupils would find it very hard to change the teacher's ideas.

> **Examiner's note** Detailed but insufficient attention to under-achievement.

Rist found the categorizing of nursery pupils began after only eight days and was based on appearance and conduct judged from middle-class values. The 'bright' children were put on the same table.

> ***Examiner's note***   Relevant study but again not focused on under-achievement.

Teachers do judge children. However, children may respond differently. Hargreaves found that children given negative labels formed their own subculture which rewarded truancy and avoided homework. Thus the teacher's judgement was detrimental.

Fuller pointed out that the teacher's judgement can be beneficial.

> ***Examiner's note***   5/8 Attempts evaluative conclusion. Answer lacks consistent focus on set question. Interactionist studies are described but not always applied to the question of under-achievement. Whether teachers' judgements are the '*main* cause of under-achievement' is not explicitly addressed.

(d) With reference to the *Items* and elsewhere, assess the view that the introduction of comprehensive schools has led to 'equal opportunity for all'. *(8 marks)*

Comprehensive schools seem to offer more equality of opportunity than the tripartite system, where children's ability was judged at eleven. We know that ability develops as children grow older and no child should be denied the opportunity to achieve.

Despite the comprehensive school being more egalitarian, inequalities based on class, gender and ethnicity still exist. Sharpe found that girls are still encouraged to do traditional female subjects such as biology and needlework rather than woodwork and science. Stanworth found that teachers devote more time in class to boys.

In spite of the overwhelming evidence, nothing has been done to improve equal opportunities. The Swann Report noted the persistence of the gulf between White and ethnic minority children.

The new right places less emphasis on equal opportunities and instead believes that the education system should serve the needs of the economy.

The National Curriculum was introduced to standardize schools and teaching methods. However, it has only served to make the system more unequal by allowing private schools not to follow the National Curriculum.

Elite theory suggests that the dominant class does not want equal oppor-tunities. They want to ensure their children will get the best education and thus the best jobs which are dominated by the privately educated.

The comprehensive school is a step in the right direction but not sufficient to produce equality of opportunity. The education system still needs to eliminate prejudice and discrimination. Parsons believed that the education system in the USA was meritocratic but Bordieu believed it still prevented the working class from succeeding.

> ***Examiner's note***   A range of knowledge here. The gender material is developed best. Reference to the *Items* would help, for example, streaming in *Item D* or the persistence of inequality because of the effects of the home (*Items B* and *C*). Refer to your notes and add some additional points both for and against comprehensive schools.
>
> Overall this answer gains 17/25.
> In order to improve, the candidate needs to demonstrate better interpretation, application and evaluation skills. You might find it useful to look at the *Items* and see if you can interpret and apply some of the evidence to the set questions, for example the comments on language in *Item B*.

4 Social stratification

★ SOLUTION TO REVISION ACTIVITY

These answers are only an indication of a suitable response. There are many other reasonable alternatives. Check with your teacher or textbook.

Produce sociological evidence and/or arguments that challenge these Marxist points of view.

1 Inequality is based solely on class differences.

Weber saw inequality as based on differences in *power*. Power could derive from *status* and *party* as well as *class*.

Functionalists argue that inequality is based on the system of differential rewards necessary to ensure that the most able people fill the functionally most important positions.

You might also focus an answer on age, ethnic and gender inequalities.

2 Class depends on ownership of the means of production.

Weber agreed with Marx that there was an upper class based on ownership of property. He also identified classes based on their different market situations. Weber was interested in *consumption* as well as *production* as the basis of inequality.

There are many schemes of social class which use occupation or consumption to distinguish classes.

Ownership of the means of production has become more widespread through individual share-holding and via institutions that invest individual's pension funds and savings.

3 There are only two significant classes.

Weber identified a growing middle class. Generally Weberians have identified a wide range of fragmented classes including an *underclass* beneath the working class.

4 Profit and wealth derive from economic exploitation.

Market theories see profit as the reward for enterprise and necessary to encourage investment, risk-taking and hard work. It is less clear how inherited wealth would encourage economic efficiency.

5 Economic 'laws' will lead to the development of class consciousness and class conflict.

Weber rejected Marx's alleged economic determinism and instead suggested that ideas could influence the economic organization of society. See Chapter 7 for a discussion of religious belief and economic change.

The fragmenting of classes and the increased emphasis on individuality in modern and postmodern societies has inhibited the development of class consciousness.

6 Marx predicted:
  ▶ Monopolization of capital.

Some firms are becoming global and tending to monopoly, for example, the 1990s mergers of drug and media corporations. However, ownership of these businesses may be more diffused. Other businesses have started up, or remained small, or demerged.

▶ Homogenization of the working class.

Weberian writers point to the fragmentation of the working classes. Divisions are found between gender and ethnic groups, native and immigrants, the more skilled and the less skilled, the employed and the unemployed.

▶ Pauperization of the working class

Some of the working class is becoming affluent not poorer.

▶ Polarization of the two classes.

Although inequality has increased since 1979 there is a substantial and growing middle class and, also, a growing gap between the working class as a whole and the poor.

7 Class conflict will lead to revolution, the triumph of the working class and the development of a classless society.

Some modern Marxists see class conflict as being prevented (for the moment) by the ideological hegemony of the ruling classes.

Pluralists see the improved living standards of the working class and the development of the Welfare State as representing a desirable alternative to a working-class revolution.

Communist revolutions took place in precapitalist societies, such as Russia, China and Cuba.

Inequalities and oppression continued in Communist societies. Most of these regimes have fallen since 1989.

ANSWERS TO EXAMINATION QUESTIONS

Question 1

(a) What does Lister mean by a 'pathological image of groups of people mentioned above' (*Item C*, line 9)? *(1 mark)*

There is a wide range of acceptable answers. The *Item* talks about disease, contamination and being different and set apart. Social pathology suggests a social problem, a condition of abnormality.

(b) Identify *one* form of social stratification, other than social class, and briefly describe its main characteristics (*Item A*). *(4 marks)*

You should identify one form and describe three main characteristics, such as age, gender, ethnicity, status, disability, occupation or caste. For example,
▶ age is socially constructed;
▶ seen as a natural difference;
▶ groups are excluded from the labour market;
▶ groups are denied political and legal rights.

(c) What sociological evidence can be presented to support the claim made in *Item B* that theories of social stratification have ignored the existence of women? *(5 marks)*

You could consider the extent to which perspectives and studies have or have not considered the existence of women.

Those explanations that rely on classifying occupations have until recently ignored the position of women. Many married women were not in paid employment, and women apparently within the same strata as men were often in lower paid occupations with few career opportunities. For example, nurses and teachers are lower paid than other professionals.

Women have often been classified according to their husband's occupations. More recent accounts have challenged this and dealt with the 'problem' of cross-class families.

Feminists have been concerned that gender stratification is found as much in the home as in the workplace and has largely been ignored in 'malestream' research.

(d) With reference to the *Items* and other sources, evaluate the Marxist account of class conflict. *(7 marks)*

Good answers will focus on *class conflict* rather than social class in general. Evaluation is essential.

Rather than just a generalized critique of Marx himself you should:
▶ question the relevance of Marx's views to contemporary society;
▶ evaluate more recent Marxist arguments and criticisms of them, such as the significance of proletarianization and embourgeoisement for the likely development of class conflict.

Your assessment should not only focus on the weaknesses of the Marxist accounts (see revision activity). You should also be aware of how modern Marxists have responded to criticisms and the continued importance of Marx's ideas in sociological debates.

(e) How far does the sociological evidence support the idea that an 'underclass' has emerged in Britain (*Item C*)? *(8 marks)*

The arguments and evidence for and against can be organized by using different theoretical perspectives:
▶ Marxists reject the idea of a separate class beneath the working class.
▶ Weberians define the underclass in terms of a lack of power. They emphasize the *structural* difference between the underclass and working class.
▶ The new right see the underclass more in *cultural* terms and take a morally disapproving view.

The different views can be seen as based on different ideologies.

They have also been used to describe different groups, such as single parents and ethnic minorities.

Critics of the whole concept have pointed out that groups and individuals drift in and out of poverty rather than form a stable class.

Question 2

(a) Give two examples of the lack of citizenship rights which may be experienced by members of ethnic minority groups (see *Item A*, line 14). *(2 marks)*

Lack of right to vote, lack of right to permanent residence or other reasonable alternatives.

(b) Give two reasons why 'more working-class than middle-class housewives have a traditional orientation to housework' (see *Item B*, lines 18–19). *(2 marks)*

Middle-class housewives tend to be better educated and have different aspirations.

Working-class extended families tend to be associated with segregated conjugal roles and reinforce traditional gender roles.

(c) Assess sociological explanations of the housewife role. *(11 marks)*

Line 12 refers to 'social-structural factors'. These have been examined by:

▶ **Marxists**, who emphasize the importance of capitalism and women's role in reproducing labour, both physically and ideologically. The housewife may also be part of a reserve army of labour.

Critics draw attention to a gendered labour market which is incompatible with the notion of a reserve army of labour.

▶ **Functionalists** see family roles as meeting the functional needs of the system. The housewife role adapts to the needs of industrial societies. Parsons distinguishes male instrumental roles from female expressive roles and sees the housewife–mother role as vital in the socialization of children.

The emergence of the symmetrical family suggests that conjugal roles are less distinct.

Critics question the existence of a more egalitarian symmetrical family and see conjugal roles as unequal rather than complementary.

▶ **Feminists**. Oakley, lines 1–2, explains the development of the housewife role by referring to industrialization which, with the development of the factory, separated work from the home. Housework is described as alienating in the language of the factory, for its monotony and isolation (lines 21–22).

Marxist–feminists emphasize the exploitation of women in the home by men as part of the overall pattern of exploitation in capitalist society.

Critics have defended housework as having some advantages over paid employment – some autonomy and perhaps a sense of fulfilment.

There are also internal debates within the feminist perspective with different attitudes to biology, Freud and Marxism.

(d) Drawing on material from *Item A* and elsewhere, assess the view that an ethnically distinct underclass exists in Britain. (*10 marks*)

Your answer should address both:
  ▶ **theoretical issues** and
  ▶ **empirical evidence**.

Marxists (lines 11–16) reject the existence of an underclass altogether and identify a single working class. The disadvantages experienced by ethnic minorities may be:

1 largely ignored (Westergaard and Resler);
2 explained in terms of the reserve army of labour (Castles and Kosack)
3 seen as a pattern of disadvantage at all levels of the working class in the form of 'racialized fractions' (Phizacklea and Miles who also introduce the issue of gender).

Weberians define the underclass in terms of their lack of power which prevents their upward mobility into a distinct working class. Giddens sees the development of 'different forms of consciousness'.

Rex and Tomlinson examined the disadvantages of immigrants in the markets for employment, housing and education which result from differences in class, status and party. Racial discrimination is an important consideration.

The new right In the USA have identified an 'ethnically distinct underclass' distinguished by their bad behaviour.

In Britain the new right has focused on welfare dependence and paid less attention to ethnic minorities.

Empirical evidence can be interpreted in different ways (lines 17–23):
  ▶ Ethnic minorities are distributed throughout the class structure.
  ▶ The experience between and within different ethnic minorities varies.
  ▶ Those from minorities who are at the bottom of the class structure are falling behind the White working class in terms of unemployment rates and pay.

Question 3 Student answer with examiner comments

(a) Which class culture does *Item C* suggest is 'classless'? (*1 mark*)

The middle class.

> **Examiner's note**   1/1 This is all that's required for the mark. Don't waste time on a fuller answer.

(b) Apart from the ways mentioned in *Item A*, suggest one other way in which the working class may be disadvantaged compared to the middle class. (*1 mark*)

Educational attainment

> **Examiner's note**   1/1/ Again a succinct answer.

(c) How far does sociological evidence support the view that the 'gap between the classes is widening' (*Item A*, line 9)? (*7 marks*)

The increase in wealth for a few is evidence that the gap is widening between the classes. Changes in taxes have advantaged the rich at the expense of the poor.

Wealth remains concentrated in the hands of a small minority. The top 1% own 20% of wealth and the top 10% over 50%. Wealth is hardly taxed and there has been a shift from direct taxation on income to indirect taxation, such as VAT, which widens the gap between the classes. However, share ownership is wider following privatization and more people own their own homes.

> **Examiner's note**   Evaluation in last sentence.

Studies of poverty have suggested an increase in those who are poor, who have been described as an underclass with a culture of dependency.

> **Examiner's note**   This could be developed.

The proportion of national earnings received by the poor has declined. In the 1980s 20% of households earned less than half average earnings and 20% earned twice average earnings.

However, the middle class is increasing in size, bridging the gap between the rich and the poor. This is caused by changes in the occupational structure as service jobs have taken over from manual jobs. The embourgeoisement thesis claims that the working class are becoming more affluent and part of an expanding middle class. This suggests that the gap between classes is not widening, although studies of voting have suggested that there is a shrinking traditional working class who remain separate from the affluent middle class.

> **Examiner's note**   Application of new knowledge, for example, on embourgeoisement and an interesting reference to voting.

Goldthorpe and Lockwood criticized the embourgeoisement theory, claiming that affluent workers formed a new working class and had not joined the middle class. Their attitudes remained working class even if incomes had risen. Eighty per cent voted Labour.

> **Examiner's note**   In 1959 perhaps, but not later.

Studies of social mobility suggest that mobility is not increasing and that the top strata of society remains closed to most people.

> **Examiner's note**   4/7 An inconsistent answer which demonstrates evaluation skills and some detailed knowledge of studies. It could be improved by using her evidence to answer more explicitly the question of the widening gap. Little use of the items and few references to theory. The candidate could also have referred to class cultures, lifestyles and attitudes, as well as to income and wealth.

(d) To what extent do sociologists agree that the modern class structure is fragmented (*Item B*)? Refer to the *Items* and other sources in your answer. (*8 marks*)

Sociologists who agree that the class structure is fragmented point out the divisions within the three main classes. These divisions may be based on different values and lifestyles. Goldthorpe and Lockwood found divisions within the working class between the old working class and the new working class who had instrumental attitudes to work and politics.

   Item B contains Roberts' view that the middle class are fragmented. He studied the class images of a wide range of white-collar employees and found that some saw themselves as working class (perhaps they voted Labour). Some saw themselves as a weak, small group compressed between powerful working and upper classes. Finally, some saw themselves as part of a large middle class and some saw themselves on a ladder of achievement rather than in a particular class.

> **Examiner's note**   Good interpretation and application of Roberts from *Items* and introduces new knowledge.

Savage, using data from the Oxford Mobility study, found three groups within the middle class. Each group had a particular type of asset. The groups were those with property assets (like Marx's *petit bourgeoisie*), those with organizational assets (such as managers) and those with cultural assets (such as a good education). Other writers on the middle class have said that there is a lower middle class of clerks. Therefore the middle class is fragmented.

> **Examiner's note**   Some detailed new knowledge and a little evaluation.

Crewe said the working class was divided into the traditional working class who live in the north, in council houses and vote Labour and the new working class who live in their own houses in the south, work in the private industries and vote Conservative.

> **Examiner's note**   Relevant, but this would be more logically placed with the other working-class material earlier in the answer.

Dahrendorf wrote about the decomposition of labour and how the working class had become divided by levels of skills and education. He also still saw divisions between the middle and working class in terms of attitudes.

   The upper class is also fragmented with division between the old aristocracy and the new entrepreneurs. They have different cultures.

> **Examiner's note**   Good interpretation of *Item C*.

> 5/8   Overall the candidate made relevant use of the *Items* and other material. There was only a limited attempt at evaluation and most of the response argued in favour of fragmentation.

(e) Assess the usefulness of the concept 'underclass' (*Item C*) in describing the social position of women.   (*8 marks*)

The underclass is a class which exists below the working class.

> **Examiner's note**   It will help to treat the term as problematic and consider different definitions.

The position of women in society has changed but the term underclass is still an appropriate description of the position of women in society today. Most part-time work is done by women and is low paid. There has been an increase in the number of single parents. Most of these are women and very many live on benefits. Giddens said women and the unemployed, who may be women, form part of the underclass. Women are seen to be dependent on males or dependent on the State. Oakley suggests that this makes them powerless.

Examiner's note   A good answer might link this reference to power to Weberian concepts of the underclass.

Lister said that the term underclass was not used in a precise way: it was too vague. Runciman and many from the new right saw the underclass as those who were dependent on the Welfare State for a long time. Single parents may be dependent but married women are not going to get benefits if they lose their jobs as they are dependent on husbands. Women have been described as part of the secondary labour market like ethnic minorities and thus part of the underclass.

On the other hand, more women are working and many are earning higher wages. Pilkington is critical of the view that women or men form a distinct underclass. Although many people recognize that women are disadvantaged in jobs, that doesn't mean they are part of the underclass. Ethnic minority women are doubly disadvantaged and the concept of the underclass is more useful in describing them.

Giddens shares the view of feminists that women are in the underclass because family responsibility reduces job opportunities. However, there are successful women with good jobs. Marxists see women as a reserve army of labour.

Examiner's note   A stronger answer would point out the differences between the underclass and the reserve army of labour.

Murray from the new right blames single mothers for their own poverty. He says the underclass behave badly rather than just have little money.

Examiner's note   6/8 An uneven performance which refers accurately to a wide range of evidence and arguments but does not always explicitly apply them to the set question. Lots of evaluation but not a clearly developed argument.

17/25 Overall a Grade A answer which displays a wide knowledge and understanding of the issues. Interpretation of the *Items* tends to be good. Answers could be better organized.

5 Poverty, welfare and social policy

Table 9 The different theories of poverty

Theory	Left wing	Right wing	Blames the individual	Blames the poor	Structural	Cultural	Blames the Welfare State
Spencer							
Culture of poverty (Lewis)		✓	✓	✓		✓	
Culture of poverty (Valentine)	✓	✓ ?	✓ ?	✓ ?	✓ structure causes culture	✓	
Marxist	✓				✓	✓	✓
Weberian (Townsend)	✓				✓		✓
Weberian (Rex)	✓				✓		
New right (Marsland)		✓	✓	✓			✓ mostly
New right (Murray)		✓	✓	✓ mostly		✓	✓
Feminist	✓				✓		✓

ANSWERS TO EXAMINATION QUESTIONS

Question 1

(a) Briefly explain what is meant by a culture of poverty. (*4 marks*)

Writers such as Lewis have claimed that the poor have distinct attitudes and patterns of behaviour which are transmitted from one generation to the next.
   The culture is generally seen as a negative influence which perpetuates poverty. Some critics accept the existence of such a culture but see it as a positive adaptation to economic conditions, rather than a culture of dependency and despair.

(b) Outline *two* problems faced by sociologists in attempting to measure the extent of poverty in contemporary society. (*4 marks*)

There is no generally agreed definition of poverty. Sociologists using absolute definitions tend to record fewer people living in poverty than those who use relative definitions.

Official statistics measure the extent of poverty by recording benefit claimants. These statistics are unreliable. They include fraudulent claimants who are not considered poor. They exclude those poor who do not qualify for benefits or do qualify but do not claim through choice or ignorance.

(c) 'Most people living in poverty are women.' Explain this statement. *(7 marks)*

You can explain the over-representation of women among the poor in a variety of ways. You do not need to develop all these points at length. Be guided by the time allowed, which is less than 15 minutes for this section. You could refer to:

▶ The large proportion of *single parent families* who are benefit-dependent. Most are female-led. This is a consequence of the social construction of a conventional feminine caring maternal role.

▶ Women are frequently *unpaid carers* of family members who are sick or have disabilities. This limits their opportunities for paid employment.

▶ The over-representation of women in *part-time and/or low-paid work*. There are a variety of sociological explanations which can be outlined here.

▶ *The distribution of resources within families*. Feminist writers, such as Graham, 1987, have argued that women get a smaller share of scarce resources than men within the family. Research evidence has shown that women may eat better after male partners have left the family home.

▶ There are more old women than men, as women live longer than men. *Old age* is related to poverty.

▶ *The benefit system* assumes that women are dependent on men and encourages this dependence.

(d) Critically assess the view that policies designed to eliminate poverty only cause increased dependency. *(10 marks)*

This section requires a coherent, logical and balanced evaluation of the view. You can include the following arguments:

▶ **New right** theorists may blame the Welfare State for poverty. Over-generous benefits are seen as creating a culture of dependence.

▶ Others from the new right may place more emphasis on the **disreputable behaviour** of the poor. This could be linked to accounts of the **culture of poverty** – which in turn perpetuates fatalism and dependency.

▶ Critics may see the **welfare system as too mean** not too generous. You can refer to the poverty trap and to claimants who cannot work.

▶ **Structuralist critics** see socially structured inequality as the cause of poverty and dependency. You can apply Marxist, Weberian or feminist approaches in a critical way to the set question.

Question 2 Student answers with examiner comments

'Some have argued that the major reasons for the continuation of poverty are the behaviour and attitudes of the poor.' Critically discuss the sociological arguments and evidence in support of this view. *(25 marks)*

New right theorists, like Marsland, believe that the attitudes of the poor cause poverty. The poor have a dependency culture created by a 'nanny state'. They have an easy life staying at home and living off the State.

> **Examiner's note**   Knowledge of the new right but some confusion here as to whether the cause of poverty is the Welfare State or the attitudes and behaviour of the poor.

However, Social Democrats believe that it is the minimal payments by the State that cause poverty. The poor do not aspire to be dependent: it imposed on them. However, Lewis argued that there was a culture of poverty and values were transmitted through the socialization process to children. Lewis was criticized by interactionists who blamed external pressures, not the attitudes and values of the poor. In fact their culture helped them to adapt to their situation of poverty.

> ***Examiner's note*** This section develops three evaluative points in a logical way. The culture of poverty is only explained in a very general way. The last criticism is not really interactionist.

Attitudes and behaviour have been a major cause of ill health in the poor, as health is closely linked to poverty. Ill health causes absence from school and work and reduces the chances of success. The working class are more likely to have dangerous jobs and thus ill health which leads to absence and loss of earnings, although safety standards have improved.

> ***Examiner's note*** Reasonable application of health material.

Many in the working class and underclass have a poor education and therefore get low paid, dead-end, dirty jobs. This means they may live in poor housing which is damp, cold and expensive to heat. However, housing benefit is available and some say it is the lack of knowledge of the poor and their desire for immediate gratification which keeps them poor, as they can't look after themselves.

> ***Examiner's note*** Some relevant knowledge but not well developed.

The lower classes tend to smoke more. This may be related to the stress of insecure employment or poverty but nevertheless it is a behavioural factor which consumes the income of the poor. It also has an adverse effect on their children which leads to a cycle of ill health and deprivation. So the behaviour of the poor can lead to poverty.

> ***Examiner's note*** New knowledge.

Social democrats explain the cycle of deprivation as the result of low benefits and unfair taxes rather than the behaviour and attitudes of the poor. Hill's research showed that between 1979 and 1986 the poorest 20% of the population have seen a decrease of 6% in their income whereas the richest 20% have shown an increase of 26%. The rich have got richer and the poor poorer as a result of changes in pay structures and the unfairness of the tax system.

> ***Examiner's note*** New knowledge of income distribution and the tax system.

Although the new right believe wealth and poverty are deserved, critics see new right policies as creating poverty. Welfare benefits are being constantly reduced and the introduction of the social fund means people only get money if they can afford to repay it. This excludes the very poor. Again it is not the attitudes and behaviour of the poor that are responsible. Mishra blames the new right for the debt culture and the no-go areas of cities which they blame on the poor.

> ***Examiner's note*** Some critical comment and further development of the debate.

Poverty is a problematic term and the poor are hard to define. Whereas Towsend found 22.9% of the population were poor, using his deprivation index Mack and Lansley found 13.8% were poor. This contrasts with government figures of 6%.

> ***Examiner's note*** Precise figures not necessary. Better to make a sociological point.

Although the government seems to see the poor as one group with inadequate values there are a variety of poor people with different attitudes and values. They are affected by how long they have been in poverty and whether they can see the end of it. The long-term poor may become hopeless and their attitudes and behaviour may encourage poverty. But this is not the case for those who see an end to poverty, such as single mothers who hope to return to work.

However, the lack of money can make it difficult to afford the clothes and fares necessary for work. So it is not attitudes but low benefits that keep people poor.

It is true that in some cases values and attitudes can cause poverty. This applies to smoking, hopelessness and unhealthy habits, but there are just as many other reasons for poverty which are forced on the poor by government policies, the Welfare State and inequality of opportunities and pay.

> **Examiner's note**   Attempts evaluative conclusion with some success. Overall the candidate has developed a series of arguments and supported them with sociological evidence. Apart from the new right there is little attempt to address theoretical issues although he does show some understanding of cultural arguments.
>
> Knowledge and understanding: *6 marks*
> Interpretation and application: *5 marks*
> Evaluation: *5 marks*
> Total: *16 marks*: grade A/B.

Question 3

Assess the argument that different definitions and explanations of poverty reflect different ideologies. *(25 marks)*

The ideological basis of different explanations of poverty is often fairly apparent. You can distinguish:
1   the ideology of the new right which emphasizes:
  ▶ individual responsibility;
  ▶ behaviour and attitudes of the poor;
  ▶ cultural explanations; and
  ▶ the over-generosity of the Welfare State.
2   the ideology of the left which emphasizes:
  ▶ socially structured inequality;
  ▶ the failure of the Welfare State to deal with poverty because of unfairness and meanness; and
  ▶ the powerlessness rather than the immorality of the underclass.
3   the ideology of feminism which emphasizes:
  ▶ the gendered nature of poverty;
  ▶ the role of men in perpetuating the poverty of women;
  ▶ structured inequality in the workplace and in the family; and
  ▶ the way in which the Welfare State perpetuates the dependence of women.
It is perhaps more difficult to see definitions as so obviously ideological. In general those definitions which minimize the number of poor are associated with the right. For example, absolute definitions rather than relative definitions. This was not always the case – the Rowntree studies identified large numbers of the absolutely poor. The right also favour definitions of poverty which suggests that the poor are different, not just lacking in money. This applies to some of the culture of poverty accounts but not to all of them.

Power and politics

Sociological theory	Marxist	Elite theory	Pluralist
Perspective	a	a	b
Source of power	a	c	b
Who holds power?	b	a	c
How do new rulers emerge?	a	b	c
The role of the State	c	b	a

 ANSWERS TO EXAMINATION QUESTIONS

Question 1

(a) Briefly outline what sociologists mean by the State. *(4 marks)*

Sociologists disagree on the definition and role of the State. The State consists of not only the government itself but also of a wide range of organizations which are agencies of government. These include the provision of health, welfare and education.

The minimal role of the State envisaged by the new right is defence of territory and the maintenance of law and order. Marxists see the State as part of the superstructure of capitalist society, maintaining existing inequalities. Weberians see the State as exercising legitimate power. Pluralists see the State as a neutral arbiter of competing interests.

(b) Using examples of each, briefly distinguish between parties and pressure groups. *(4 marks)*

Political parties are usually broad coalitions of interests who combine to seek power and form a government. The major political parties in Britain are the Conservative and Labour Parties.

Pressure groups have narrower aims. They may be committed to a single issue, such as banning the export of live animals. They may alternatively represent the interests of a section of society such as employers, workers or the old. Pressure groups try to influence governments rather than seek electoral victory.

(c) Outline the elitist theory of power. *(7 marks)*

Elites are the small minority at the top of a particular aspect of social life. Elite theories of power focus on governing elites. They may also refer to economic or military power (C. W. Mills).

Elite theories have a constant-sum view of power. Power is concentrated, held by the minority and exercised in their own interests.

Elite theories are a critical alternative to Marxism. They neither see ownership as the sole source of power nor the class struggle as the only cause of political change. Elite rule is seen as inevitable and, by some, as desirable. A Communist revolution will not lead to the withering away of the State.

You may wish to refer to a variety of elite theories including:

- ► Classical theories: Mosca, Pareto, Michels;
- ► The power elite: C. W. Mills; and
- ► Elite pluralism/fragmented elites: Marsh, Richardson, Jordan.

(d) Assess the strengths and weaknesses of the pluralist theory of power. *(10 marks)*

To achieve a high grade you must offer a balanced evaluation where both strengths and weaknesses are assessed. A juxtaposition of pluralism with alternatives such as Marxism or the elite theory will not score high marks. Explicit evaluation is required. Two marks are reserved for presenting a logical and coherent account that focuses on the set question.

You could assess some of the following points:

Strengths

- ► explain how political decisions may favour the weak as well as the strong;
- ► explain the roles of political parties and pressure groups in the political system;
- ► provide a critical alternative to the existence of elites or ruling classes who are said to dominate society;
- ► encourage empirical examination of the nature and distribution of power by analysing decision-making;
- ► fit the doctrine of the separation of powers found in American political institutions; and
- ► show awareness of the variety of identities, groups and interests in fragmented contemporary society. Gender, age, ethnicity, beliefs are potential influences on political interests, not just class.

Weaknesses

- ► concentrate exclusively on political power rather than economic power;
- ► only examine the first face of power i.e. decision-making;
- ► does not consider the ability of the powerful to avoid the consideration of issues that threaten them;
- ► some weak groups are not represented by parties or pressure groups; and
- ► some parties and interest groups are much more powerful than others.

You may refer to:

- ► pluralists such as Dahl;
- ► Marx and Marxists such as Lukes, Miliband and Marcuse; and
- ► elite theorists.

Question 2 Student answer with examiner comments

Compare and contrast Marxist and new right perspectives on the role of the State in society. *(25 marks)*

Marxist and new right theorists come from the two extremes of social thinking. Therefore it is not surprising that they differ on the role of the State in society.

Marxists argue that the State serves the interests of the ruling class in capitalist societies. The State helps to maintain the exploitation which is an essential feature of capitalism.

The new right has the opposite view of capitalism. It is seen as producing high standards of living for most of the population and also, according to Hayek, is the only economic system which allows for freedom of the individual.

Examiner 's note   Clear contrast between two views of capitalism.

The new right believe that the role of the State should be minimal. This will encourage individual independence and freedom. They particularly believe that State intervention in the economy should be minimal, as such intervention interferes with the efficient working of market forces and a less competitive economy. Thus new right theorists support a society where there is a large degree of personal freedom in both the political and economic spheres. This will produce more democracy and prosperity. The wealth created by capitalism freed from State intervention is thought to 'trickle down' to the poor.

Marxists fundamentally disagree with this view of the role of the State in capitalist society. They see non-intervention in the economy as simply perpetuating the exploitation of the weak. The minimal State allows the gap between the rich and poor to widen.

> *Examiner 's note* Opportunity here to refer to the debate over the Welfare State.

Marxists see the State as playing a major role in capitalist society. They do not approve of this role which is to protect those who have economic power. The State uses force to prevent a revolution. It controls the army and the police who act on behalf of the ruling class, not the people as a whole.

After the Communist revolution predicted by Marx, the State will eventually wither away, as it will have no role to play in a classless society.

> *Examiner 's note* She could point out the similarity with the new right aim of a minimalist State.

However, in a capitalist society Marxists would like the State to play a major role but different from the way they see it operating at present. The desirable role would involve massive economic intervention through nationalization and regulation to reduce the effects of exploitation.

It should be noted that such an economic role has not led to economic success in Marxist-based Communist societies in Eastern Europe. Such societies were economic failures compared to the West: they may have been more egalitarian but living standards fell. Also in such societies the State has curbed political and human rights.

Marxist critics of such Communist States saw them as dictatorships rather than classless societies. They were not really based on Marxist principles.

> *Examiner 's note* The candidate has demonstrated a good understanding of both the Marxist and new right perspectives. There are explicit attempts to compare and contrast the two views.
>
> There is a lack of references to sociological sources. The best answers might address the 'internal' Marxist debates referring to Miliband, Poulantzas, Gramsci and Althusser. She might also refer to other topics she has studied to illustrate new right views on, say, the Welfare State, the family or education.
>
> Knowledge and understanding: *6 marks*
> Interpretation and application: *5 marks*
> Evaluation: *5 marks*
> Total: *16 marks*: grade A/B.

Question 3

To what extent has the concept of the 'deviant voter' been relevant and useful in sociological accounts of voting behaviour? *(25 marks)*

To gain high marks candidates will have to move beyond the mere description of a 'shopping list' of studies of deviant voting.

It is necessary to explore both theoretical and empirical aspects of the question by examining the extent to which the concept of deviant voting is compatible with various explanations of voting behaviour.

1 When social class and political socialization were seen as the dominant explanations of voting, the concept of 'deviant voting' became useful.
It helped explain the success of right-wing parties not only in Britain but in other industrialized societies where there was a majority of manual workers. These were seen as working class and thus likely to vote for left-wing parties.
   The explanations of deviant voting included:
   ▶ McKenzie and Silver, who distinguished deferential and secular working-class Tory voters; and
   ▶ Parkin who focuses on ideology (dominant, subordinate and radical value systems) to explain both working-class Tories and middle-class Labour voters. He redefines the notion of 'deviance' to cover only Labour voters.

2 Deviant voting is closely related to the development of ideas of class and partisan dealignment. Such ideas, which lead on to the importance of 'consumer choice', would ultimately make the idea of deviance redundant. If there is no general rule of class loyalty to parties, there are no rulebreaking deviant voters to explain.

3 Theories that argue for changes in the class structure do not rely on the concept of deviant voters although they may help explain so-called deviant voting.
   Studies identifying a *fragmented class structure* include:
   ▶ Rose (1968) on the working class;
   ▶ Goldthorpe (1978) on the middle class; and
   ▶ Heath *et al.* and their five classes.
   Changes such as *embourgeoisement* (in its 1950s or 1990s versions) would explain deviant working-class voting, although critics (Goldthorpe *et al.* in the 1960s and Devine in the 1990s) have challenged the embourgeoisement thesis.

7 Religion

Assessment		
Evidence	*For secularization*	*Against secularization*
Decline in church attendance	Religious behaviour is in decline.	Attendance is not essential for some religions. Observation has become an individual matter.
Decline in other forms of participation, such as dietary rules, rites of passage	Religion is losing its significance. Continuation of 'religious' behaviour is customary.	First marriages are often religious. Reasons for behaviour in the past were often customary, not religious.
Disengagement of Church from State	Religion is losing political and moral influence. Loss of educational, welfare, political and social control functions.	Structural differentiation means Church is 'purer'. Continuation of Protestant tradition of individualism. The emergence and persistence of religious political movements and States.
Growing acceptance of scientific/rational thinking	Disenchantment and desacrilization. Belief in the sacred and supernatural have declined. The development of 'modern' society undermines traditional religious thinking.	Rise of fundamentalism. Popularity of 'new age' and other irrational beliefs. A wide variety of beliefs exist in postmodern societies.
Decline in traditional moral behaviour, such as acceptance of divorce, abortion and homosexuality	Religious institutions and thinking are losing influence. Where 'new morality' is accepted by Churches it indicates the secularization of those institutions.	Religious beliefs and institutions are adapting rather than in decline. Religious morality has been 'generalized' to wider society.
Growth of new religious movements	The loss of a monopoly of truth undermines the influence of all religion. Sects are the 'last outpost' of religion in secular society.	Indicates change rather than decline. Sects often offer 'purer' religion.

ANSWERS TO EXAMINATION QUESTIONS

Question 1 **Student answer with examiner comments**
'The main function of religion in society is the control of weaker social groups by the more powerful.' Evaluate sociological arguments both for and against this statement. *(25 marks)*

The assertion that religion in capitalist society is used as a means of control is a Marxist one. Marxists such as Althusser argue that religion is an ideological state apparatus – a means by which the working class are indoctrinated with ideas.

Religion is seen as means of control, for example, poverty is viewed as a virtue by Christians. People in powerful positions are thought to be ordained by God and social inequality is said to be determined by God.

Thus Marxists argue that religion maintains a false consciousness. It is the 'opiate of the people', keeping them oppressed and hiding inequality.

> **Examiner's note** Clearly states a Marxist perspective. Accurate knowledge of Althusser and relevant application of points on poverty and false consciousness. Needs to be more fully developed.

The Marxist view has been criticized by functionalists. They argue that the main function of religion is to create a consensus of values and maintain social cohesion.

> **Examiner's note** Rather simplistic criticism. There is no direct reference to the question – only an alternative to Marxism.

Both Marxist and functionalist views have been criticized by sociological evidence. The civil rights movement in the USA used both Christianity and Islam to help the struggle for equal rights. This directly criticizes the Marxist view that religion only serves the needs of the more powerful.

> **Examiner's note** Example critically applied to the set question.

Religion-based conflicts in Northern Ireland and Bosnia highlight weaknesses in the functionalist view that religion is a cohesive force. However, functionalists may argue that each side is bound by loyalty to that religion.

> **Examiner's note** Attempts evaluation without direct reference to control of the weak by the strong.

Both Marxists and functionalists argue that religion is a form of social control. Marxists see this as a negative thing supporting exploitation whereas functionalists argue it is positive, encouraging consensus.

> **Examiner's note** Compares the two theories and refers to control.

Weberians argue that religion can initiate social change. Weber rejected Marxist economic determinism. He described how Calvinism encouraged the rise of capitalism. The Protestant ethic encouraged the accumulation of wealth and individualism.

> **Examiner's note** Potentially relevant but not used to answer the question.

Marxists argued that the Protestant ethic legitimized free enterprise and thus religion helps the exploitation of the weak working class by the powerful ruling class.

> **Examiner's note** Effective assessment of Weber applied to set question.

The relationship between the main function of religion and weaker or powerful groups is a complex one. Bellah rejects the view that religion must always be seen in structuralist terms and emphasizes individual religiosity. Religion affects members of society in different ways; it is not always a form of social control of the weak, for example, the civil rights movements of the 1960s.

> *Examiner 's note*   Reasonable attempt at evaluative conclusion.

Feminists have suggested that gender influences the function of religion as religion leigitimizes patriarchy.

> *Examiner 's note*   Rather isolated final point which could be developed to gain more marks.
>
> Overall, a competent answer considering the time constraints of examination conditions.
>
> He does make consistent attempts to apply the three main theories to the set question and is also trying to evaluate arguments and evidence where posible.
>
> Knowledge and understanding: *5 marks*
> Interpretation and application: *5 marks*
> Evaluation: *5 marks*
> Total: *15 marks:* a B grade answer.

Question 2

(a) Identify *two* features of secularization. *(4 marks)*

A decline in religious practice, such as few people attending religious services.
A decline in the influence of religious institutions over everyday life, such as education.

(b) Identify and illustrate *two* criticisms of the secularization theseis. *(4 marks)*

Sociologists do not agree on the definition of the concept of secularization.
Sociologists do not agree on the degree of religiosity that existed in the past so that the necessary comparison with the present is problematic.

(c) Outline the evidence for the secularization of the UK. *(7 marks)*

Relevant sociological evidence should be related to the theoretical arguments.
You could use Wilson's distinction between:
- ▶ **belief**
- ▶ **practice** and
- ▶ **institutions**

as a framework for your answer. Reference to concepts such as disenchantment and disengagement may help but don't try to answer question (d) in this section!

(d) Examine the reasons for the changes in institutional religion in the UK. *(10 marks)*

'Examine the reasons' is instructing you to use your evaluation skills and assess the relevant evidence and arguments.
You could include discussion of:
- ▶ the alleged growth of scientific thinking and rationalism in modern societies. Refer to Weber and disenchantment, for example.
- ▶ the disengagement of the Church from social life; and Parsons' arguments about structural differentiation;
- ▶ the development of religious pluralism that undermines the 'universe of meaning'; and
- ▶ the arguments about the individuation of belief and practice.

Question 3

Critically examine the sociological contributions to an understanding of the relationship between religion and social change in society. *(25 marks)*

There is a wide range of evidence and arguments that can be critically examined here.

The main sociological debate could be organized around the argument between Marx and Weber.

Marxists see religion as a part of the superstructure of societies. As such, religion is shaped by the economic infrastructure and will change in response to changes in the economic organization of society. Religious beliefs and institutions will help to reproduce the existing relations of production i.e. the exploitative class system. Thus religion is seen as inhibiting social change by legitimizing inequality and keeping the potentially revolutionary working class in a state of false consciousness.

In contrast, Weber sees the possibility of ideas and beliefs shaping the economic organization of society. In particular he explains how the 'Protestant ethic' was associated with the rise of capitalism.

Both the Marxist and Weberian views can be supported by reference to subsequent sociological evidence or social events.

Ensure that references to functionalism are applied to the set question and are not just descriptions of theory and studies. Functionalism is usually seen as suggesting that religion is essentially a conservative force.

A more broadly based account could refer to discussion of the significance of the:

▶ feminist perspectives on religion;
▶ rise of new religious movements as a response to social change; and
▶ decline in the influence of religion in the wake of a more rational modern society.

8 Deviance, crime and social control

	Functionalist	*Interactionist*
1 Perspective	b	a
2 Research approach	a	b
3 Definition of deviance	a	b
4 Attitude to police and courts	b	a
5 Attitude to crime statistics	a d	b c
6 Major criticisms	a b d e	b c d

ANSWERS TO EXAMINATION QUESTIONS

The relationship between ethnicity and deviance is clearly a sensitive issue and it may be difficult for many students and teachers to remain objective. Few answers uncritically accept the higher reported rates for (some) crimes among (some) ethnic groups but there is often a tendency to accept a crude view of a racist criminal justice system as the answers to any question on this topic.

Your best option is cite sociological evidence and show your awareness of conflicting explanations, such as new criminology versus new left realism.

Question 1

(a) Briefly outline what sociologists mean by a 'moral panic'. *(4 marks)*

A moral panic occurs when there is a sudden and significant public demand that something should be done about what has become defined as a social problem. The social problem may be objectively real and just discovered and publicized by the media; or imaginary and invented by the media. Erikson wrote about the moral panic over witches in seventeenth-century America and explained it from a functionalist point of view. There has often been an element of witch-hunting in subsequent moral panics. The concept of deviance amplification is often related to moral panics.

(b) Briefly identify and illustrate *two* aspects of the relationship between ethnicity and crime in the UK. *(4 marks)*

Ethnic minorities have been identified as both the perpetrators and victims of certain types of crime.

Black youth have been labelled as 'muggers' on more than one occasion by the police and media.

Asians have been particularly identified as victims of racist attacks.

(c) Outline the weaknesses suggested by sociologists in the police statistics on the relationship between ethnic groups and crime. *(7 marks)*

You should cover both theoretical and empirical criticisms. Don't develop arguments which will be used to answer part (d).

Interactionists have argued that official statistics are a social construction that tell us more about the people and processes involved in their collection and analysis than about the phenomena they claim to describe. The police and media are seen as having a major role in the social construction of crime statistics.

Marxists, such as Hall and, later, Gilroy, have used the interactionist perspective to explain the labelling of Black 'offenders' within the context of capitalist society. On the one hand they argue that political resistance may be labelled as Black crime and on the other they deny that offenders are more likely to be Black and the statistics are the product of racism in the police force and the rest of the criminal justice system.

Even those who have a more positivist approach to crime have suggested that crime figures may be unreliable. They demonstrate this by comparing crimes known to the police with other statistical sources such as victim studies and self-report studies.

(d) Examine the claim that 'popular' views of Black criminality are 'myths'. *(10 marks)*

This needs a balanced and sensitive evaluation of the work of:

▶ those who dismiss higher conviction rates or media myths about crime as having no objective foundation, such as the new criminology, Hall, and Gilroy;
▶ the response to this view in the later work of Young in his New Left Realism;
▶ older research and theories can be applied to the issue of Black crime, either explaining it in terms of anomie or subculture, or used to dismiss it by referring to interactionist theories.

Question 2
Examine critically the relationship between deviance and power. *(25 marks)*

This is a general question for which there is a wide variety of legitimate responses.

The answer can be organized around a theoretical framework. *You are not expected to go through every approach to deviance that you know.*

You should select theories that contribute to a balanced and evaluative answer.

The most obvious approaches to apply to the question are:

▶ **Marxist**
▶ **interactionist**

▶ and their later developments such as:

▶ **New Criminology**
▶ **New Left Realism.**

However, it is equally useful, if more difficult, to apply:

► **functionalism**
► **feminism**.

For each theory you could consider:

► Who are seen as the powerful?
► Can the powerful define what is deviant?
► Do the powerful influence the enforcement of rules?
► How can the powerful avoid being processed as deviant?

Better answers will show an understanding of more complex issues such as competing definitions of deviance and power. They will probably discuss the relationship between inequality, power and deviance.

Read the question a few times while planning an answer. This question asks about *deviance*, not just *crime*. Therefore a complete answer will at least refer to other kinds of deviance, such as interactionist views on mental illness or feminist views on patriarchal definitions of deviant feminine behaviour.

Question 3 Student answer with examiner comments

'Many sociological approaches to deviance have ignored the extent to which females are involved in crime.' Discuss the evidence and arguments for and against this view. *(25 marks)*

> *Examiner's note*   Although knowledge and understanding of feminist studies of crime may figure prominently in a good answer, they are not sufficient. There must be some evaluation of 'malestream' theories to see if they do indeed neglect female involvement in crime. Victims, as well as 'offenders', may be discussed.

Official crime statistics show that women do not commit as much crime as men. Men are shown to commit five times as much crime although women are more likely to be shoplifters. Because they use official statistics, sociologists have tended to concentrate on working-class males rather than females.

> *Examiner's note*   Simple but effective application of reason for disregarding female involvement in crime.

Heidensohn is a feminist sociologist who believes that many sociologists have neglected the study of females for many reasons. First, because of vicarious identification, males have preferred to study male crime. Second, deviance is a male-dominated subject where teachers and researchers are male even if students are mostly female. Thus researchers have been more interested in male crime. Third, Heidensohn argues that the lower recorded crime rates have discouraged the study of female crime. For example, Thrasher's study of gangs identified only one female gang in the midst of hundreds of male gangs. Finally, Heidensohn said that before the development of feminist perspectives there were no adequate explanations of female crime.

> *Examiner's note*   Heidensohn is used to answer the set question.

There are critics of Heidensohn and the view stated in the question. Some sociologists see women as under-represented in the crime statistics: they commit much less crime because of the way they are socialized. Girls are socialized to be caring and domesticated, not aggressive like boys. McRobbie and Garber said that girls have developed a 'bedroom culture' at home while boys are out on the streets. Thus girls lack the opportunity to commit crime when teenagers and as this is the peak period for crime they commit less and do not grow up as criminals. Married women also spend a lot of time at home.

Examiner's note   Alternative point of view offered and developed
following an evaluative comment which helps to create an evaluative
framework.

Many of the traditional theories of crime ignore females. Merton and the
subcultural theorists like Cohen, Miller, and Cloward and Ohlin, all saw crime
as a male working-class phenomenon.

Examiner's note   This could have been developed. Critical comment is
accurate and the point concerning the focus on the male working class is
made relevant.
A critical mention of girl gangs would help.

Pollack claimed that female crime figures were low because women concealed
their crimes, for example, prostitution. Female crime can be unmasked by
self-report studies. Campbell found very similar levels of male and female
crime using this method, although boys still reported slightly more than girls.
Box said that the gap between male and female crime was still great if only
serious crimes were studied.

Examiner's note   A new and relevant explanation is offered and
developed with appropriate references.

In conclusion we have seen that sociologists who rely on the official crime
statistics have often chosen to ignore female crime. Others who rely on their
own research, such as Campbell and Heidensohn, have found evidence of
female crime. Official crime statistics have been criticized for being invalid and
unreliable. There is much unrecorded crime. Kalven has argued that the
police and the courts act chivalrously and this prevents female crime from
leading to conviction and being recording in the statistics, although recent
murder convictions for women who have killed husbands who abused them
question this view.

Recent explanations of female crime have concentrated on the reasons for
the low rate of female crime, such as McRobbie. But the statement in the
question is right: many approaches have ignored women.

Although knowledge and understanding of feminist studies of crime may
figure prominently in a good answer, they are not sufficient. There must be
some evaluation of 'malestream' theories to see if they do indeed neglect
female involvement in crime. Victims as well as 'offenders' may be discussed.

Examiner's note   The conclusion introduces some new critical comments,
for example, on the chivalrous treatment of women. Previous arguments
are summarized in a critical way. The last paragraph demonstrates she
understands the question is not just about females and crime but also how
sociologists have dealt with this subject.

Overall this answer, although not always completely developed, is full of
relevant and accurate knowledge. The answer is well-organized with a
clear and coherent argument developed throughout the essay. Evaluation
is present both in terms of specific points and a relevant debate running
through the answer.

Knowledge and understanding: *7 marks*
Interpretation and application: *6 marks*
Evaluation: *6 marks*
Total: *19 marks*: a clear grade A.

part IV
Timed practice papers with answers

⭐ EXAM TIPS

In this final part of the *Exam Practice Kit* you should practise your examination skills in as realistic setting as possible. You need to find a quiet room where you will not be interrupted for the duration of the test. You should be quite strict about keeping to the prescribed time for the whole of a paper.

The time allowed to complete any examination is not only for the writing of answers but also any for any reading and thinking time. You can help to use the limited time efficiently by being as familiar as possible with the layout and rubric (the set of instructions at the start of the paper) of the examination papers for your syllabus.

You can get this information from the syllabus, specimen papers and usually past papers. Remember to be fully informed about any new developments in the content or structure of syllabuses and examination papers.

You should ensure that the marks allocated to a part of a question influence how much time you spend on it and thus how long your answer is. Chief examiners' reports often refer to candidates who write long discursive answers to questions worth four marks and then have insufficient time to develop the more essay-type of answers required when eight or more marks are allocated.

Question papers

Time allowed: 2 hours.
Answer *two* questions.

▶ Mark allocations are shown for each question.
▶ You are reminded of the need for good English and clear presentation in your answers.
▶ You are advised to spend an equal amount of time on each question.

Question 1   Theory and Methods

Item A

Most discussions of research in sociology put their main emphasis on field-work, survey research or a combination of the two. Documentary research – the systematic use of printed or written materials for investigation – is often regarded as second best. Yet there are very few pieces of field-work or survey research which do not involve some scrutiny of documentary material. Documentary research, in one guise or another, is in fact one of the most widely used of all methods of gathering sociological data.

Some of the documents most often consulted in sociological research are public and private records, for example: government documents, church records, letters or judicial records. The documents used in research virtually always also include information and findings produced by previous writers in the field in question. Many investigations are as much concerned with collecting together and analysing materials from the work of others as with generating wholly new data.

Adapted from *Sociology*, A. Giddens (Polity 1989)

Item B: Rates of suicide for selected countries as used by Durkheim

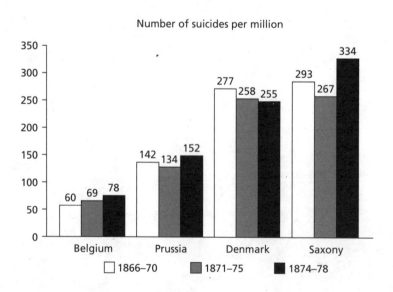

Number of suicides per million

Source: adapted from E. Durkheim, *Le Suicide*, 1897

Item C

When looking at secondary data, positivists tend to emphasize official documentation and statistics as the most reliable. For example, they might point to death rates as 'hard' data – that is, data in which there is little opportunity for error or subjectivity to affect the 'truth' of the information. As there is a legal requirement to record deaths, the positivists argue that such data fulfil the conditions for qualification as 'scientific' information.

In using secondary data, anti-positivists turn to accounts which participants have recorded themselves, such as diaries, letters and even novels, and they adopt a critical stance towards them. There are thousands of 'life-documents' now available to sociologists, through which they may explore the cultures and subcultures of a society. While accepting that such documents are inevitably biased and subjective, they argue that, with careful handling, they can peel back the surface appearances of society and reveal the *lebenswelt* – the day-to-day and minute-by-minute activities of the millions of people who make up what we call society.

(a) Which country showed a consistent decline in the suicide rate between 1866 and 1878 (*Item B*)? *(1 mark)*
(b) Give *two* other examples, other than death rates, of 'hard' statistics (*Item C*). *(2 marks)*
(c) In what ways have sociologists been critical of the use of official statistics, such as those used by Durkheim (*Item B*)? *(7 marks)*
(d) Using material from the *Items* and elsewhere, assess the usefulness of secondary data, other than official statistics, as sources of information. *(8 marks)*
(e) Assess the factors which affect whether researchers choose to examine 'hard' data or life-documents (*Item C*). *(7 marks)* (AEB, 1994)

Question 2 Family

Item A

Functionalists would interpret male superiority in terms of the more significant roles males play in the fulfilment of certain societal needs: their greater role in war, in government, in the economy and in ceremonials that promote social solidarity and cohesiveness. They believe that the higher the skill and responsibility of the man in extra-familial roles, the greater is the effective superiority of the husband in family decision-making.

According to the Marxist model, male superiority arises from, and is related to, control of private property by males. Frederick Engels traced an evolutionary pattern in husband–wife relationships that corresponded to stages of economic development. The earliest stages, where property was communal, were characterized by the relatively unstable matings of group marriage and temporary pairings. Women's status was not only high, it was 'supreme', because the biological fathers of offspring could not be identified and because in the communistic household, the administration of the household was seen as a socially necessary industry.

Source: adapted from B. Yoburg, *Families & Societies*, Columbia University Press

Item B

There has been a growing acceptance among sociologists that childhood, like so many other vitally important aspects of social life – gender, health, youth and so on – was socially constructed. It was, in other words, what members of particular societies, at particular times and in particular places, said it was.

This has two implications:

1 Childhood is a social construction. It isn't natural and should be distinguished from biological immaturity.
2 Childhood varies, both in relation to class, gender and ethnicity and across national cultures. There is no single universal childhood.

Source: adapted from Stephen Wagg, *Sociology Review*, Vol. 1, no. 4, 1992

Item C

As many as one in five families with dependent children are now headed by a lone parent. This covers about 1.3 million parents living with 2.1 million children. Two per cent of all households in Britain are headed by a lone father, a figure which has been fairly stable in recent years. Lone mothers head 18 per cent of all households, but here there has been a marked increase over the last few years. Jo Roll argues that whereas the general increase in one-parent families over the last decade could be attributed to rising divorce and and separation rates, 'In Britain in the late 1980s there also seems to have been an increase in the number of younger unmarried women deciding to have children and living alone without their partners'.

Source: adapted from Martyn Denscombe, *Sociology Update*, 1993

Item D

Social Security Secretary, Peter Lilley, wrote: 'We have produced a generation of fatherless children. No father to support them, discipline them and set them an example.' He claimed that the rise in violent crime since 1950 was largely caused by the increasing absence of fathers in families. He is wrong. The overwhelming scientific evidence shows that neither illegitimacy nor the absence of fathers causes these children to grow up more violent than those raised by couples, married or otherwise.

Source: adapted from Oliver J. Vicious, 'Outcome of the poverty trap', *Observer*, 23 May 1993

(a) What is the total percentage of households in Britain headed by a lone parent of either gender (*Item C*)? *(1 mark)*
(b) *Item A* gives reasons suggested by functionalists and Marxists for 'male superiority' in the family. Give *two* criticisms of this functionalist view and *two* criticisms of this Marxist view. *(4 marks)*
(c) How might a feminist explain 'male superiority' in the family (*Item A*)? *(5 marks)*
(d) Using examples, discuss the extent to which sociologists agree that childhood is a social construction (*Item B*). *(7 marks)*
(e) With reference to *Items C* and *D*, and other sources, assess sociological contributions to an understanding of lone-parent families. *(8 marks)* (AEB, 1995)

Question 3   Education

Item A

Hargreaves (*Social Relations in a Secondary School*) observed the normative structure of the pupils in their forms in a secondary modern school. He was concerned with the significance of the peer group in regulating patterns of behaviour. Teachers tended to assume that negative behaviour could be explained in terms of 'bad home-background'. Hargreaves argues that this is an oversimplification. It ignores the crucial aspect of the pupils' subcultures as these develop in the process of classroom interaction. The subcultures tended to relate to the form the pupils were in and their stream. Pupils in the top streams had more positive attitudes than those in the lowest.

Source: P. Selfe, *Advanced Sociology*, Pan

Item B

Sharp and Green identify three pupil types. First, there are the 'ideal' pupils, the bright, easily controlled minority, who are self-motivated and need little of the teacher's time and attention; they can 'get on' on their own. These pupils are easily understood and identified with; their behaviour and their few learning problems 'make sense' to the teacher. Second, there are the majority of 'normal' pupils. These take up most of the teacher's time, but again their problems are not difficult to understand or deal with. With help they can be kept busy and do not require a lot of thinking about. Third, there are the few 'problem' children, who are often regarded as 'peculiar' or disturbed. One strategy for coping with these pupils, which Sharp and Green observed, involved removing them from the mainstream of classroom activities and allowing them to spend time playing in the Wendy House. Here Sharp and Green attempt to link classroom practice at the micro-level with the reproduction of class relations within society generally.

Source: adapted from S. Ball, *Education*, Longman

Item C

As a group, Afro–Caribbean women are among the best-educated women in Britain, with 37 per cent gaining A-level qualifications or above, compared with 31 per cent of white women and much lower levels in other ethnic groups.

However, a recent Policy Studies Institute (PSI) report on the position of Britain's ethnic minorities shows that secondary education is all too often where the black female success story ends. According to the report, 23 per cent of white women educated to A-level standard or above are in professional or managerial positions, compared with only 16 per cent of Afro–Caribbean women with the same qualifications.

Source: M. Forma and L. Pilkington, 'Jobs for the boys (and the white girls)',
Guardian, 3 June 1993

Item D

From the concern expressed during the 1950s and 1960s about working-class under-achievement, a number of programmes of compensatory education were developed. These were designed to counter disadvantage by providing educational resources which would ensure that wastage would be eliminated and equality achieved. The programmes were based on the assumption that the culture of the deprived was in some way 'deficient' or lacking in such areas as attitudes to education, language and child-rearing patterns.

Source: adapted from C. Court, *Basic Concepts in Sociology*, Checkmate

(a) By how many percentage points do Afro–Caribbean women outperform white women in gaining A-level qualifications or above (*Item C*)? *(1 mark)*

(b) Name *two* programmes of compensatory education (*Item D*). *(2 marks)*

(c) Assess the importance of pupils' subcultures in influencing educational attainment (*Items A* and *B*). *(7 marks)*

(d) With reference to *Item C* and other information, evaluate sociological contributions to an understanding of the educational achievement of ethnic minorities in Britain. *(8 marks)*

(e) To what extent do sociologists agree with the idea that compensatory education programmes (*Item D*) have helped pupils from 'bad home-backgrounds' (*Item A*)? *(7 marks)*

(AEB, 1995)

Question 4 Stratification

Item A

In a recent article, Vaughan Robinson of Swansea University reviews the social mobility of British blacks. He uses data derived from the Longitudinal Study of the Office of Population and Censuses to track the mobility of individuals between the 1971 and 1981 census.

Robinson commences by reviewing the picture revealed in previous studies, especially the two well-known Policy Studies Institute works by Smith (1977) and Brown (1984). Smith's data showed widespread downward mobility for newly arrived members of ethnic minorities, qualified individuals often being forced to take manual, including unskilled manual, work. Brown's later study showed some improvement with all ethnic minorities increasing their representation in white-collar occupations. However, much of this was in routine white-collar work and accountable through occupational change rather than increased opportunities for individual mobility. Moreover, most had not managed to reproduce the class position of themselves or their parents prior to arrival in Britain. This point was confirmed by Heath and Ridge's 1983 analysis of the Nuffield Social Mobility data which showed that 50 per cent of the sample were from *petit bourgeois* or farm-owning backgrounds originally but were now concentrated in the working class.

Source: Dave Wells, 'Gleanings', *Social Science Teacher 20*, 2, Spring 1991

Item B

Social background of university full-time students in 1989–90

Social group	% in population	% in universities
I	10	20
II	29	50
III (non-manual)	9	11
III (manual)	36	12
IV	11	6
V	4	1

(UCCA)

Item C

There is a current debate in sociology about the significance of class identity. Some, like Gordon Marshall, adhere to the view that class identity has far from disappeared. Levels of social mobility and the degree of social closure affect the homogeneity of social classes and hence the importance of class identity for their members. John Goldthorpe has recently indicated that the expansion of the 'service' class, and therefore its recruitment of individuals from other classes, might mean a weakening in the class identity of that class. However, he argues that the class identity of the working class remains strong. This is because it has a high level of self-recruitment (four out of five male manual workers have manual workers as fathers) and because its diminishing size and influence have made it more concentrated and solid. A similar point might be made about upper-class identity, where there is also a high level of self-recruitment.

Source: Jane Clarke and Carol Saunders, *Sociology Review*, Vol. 1, no. 1, September 1991

(a) According to *Item B* what is the difference between the percentage of full-time university students from Social Class I and the percentage from Social Class V? *(1 mark)*

(b) What do sociologists mean by the statement that increased mobility is the result of 'occupational change rather than increased opportunities for individual mobility' (*Item A*)? *(2 marks)*

(c) In what ways do sociologists believe that levels of social mobility affect the importance of class identity (*Item C*)? *(4 marks)*

(d) With reference to the *Items* and elsewhere, assess the argument that there is still a high level of self-recruitment in the British class structure. *(9 marks)*

(e) With reference to *Item A* and other sources, evaluate sociological explanations of the class position of ethnic minorities. *(9 marks)*

(AEB, 1994)

Timed practice paper 2

Time allowed: 1 hour 30 minutes
Answer *two* questions.

▶ Mark allocations are shown for each question.
▶ You are reminded of the need for good English and clear presentation in your answers.
▶ You are advised to spend an equal amount of time on each question.

Question 1   Politics
Evaluate the claim made by some sociologists that there is a 'dominant ideology' in modern capitalist societies. *(25 marks)*

(AEB, 1995)

Question 2   Religion
'Durkheim's view that religion reinforces the collective conscience of society is more appropriate to an understanding of small, non-literate societies, than it is to large, modern and diversified societies.' Critically examine this argument. *(25 marks)*

(AEB, 1995)

Question 3   Poverty
Assess the sociological evidence for and against the argument that the Welfare State both creates and perpetuates a culture of dependency. *(25 marks)*

(AEB, 1995)

Question 4   Deviance
'The usefulness of crime statistics in sociological research depends on the theoretical approach adopted by the sociologist.' Critically explain this view. *(25 marks)*

(AEB, 1996)

Answers to timed practice paper 1

You should have read all the parts of the question before you attempt your answers. It is worth looking again to decide in which part of the question it is most appropriate to develop particular points.

Question 1   Theory and methods
(a) Which country showed a consistent decline in the suicide rate between 1866 and 1878 (*Item B*)? *(1 mark)*

Denmark (Note that a full sentence is not required.)

(b) Give *two* other examples, other than death rates, of 'hard' statistics (*Item C*). *(2 marks)*

Birth rates. Divorce rates.

(c) In what ways have sociologists been critical of the use of official statistics, such as those used by Durkheim (*Item B*)? *(7 marks)*

This part can be answered using both the framework and many of the ideas found in the crime statistics question in Paper 2.

1 *Positivists* who approve of Durkheim's use of official statistics to develop and test hypotheses may have reservations about their:
   ► **reliability**;
   ► **completeness**; and
   ► **representativeness**.
You can develop and illustrate these and other points by referring to the incompleteness of figures of crimes known to the police or the reliability of unemployment figures when definitions change.

2 *Interpretive sociologists* question the *validity* of (suicide and other) statistics. They are seen as socially constructed by the commonsense assumptions of coroners, police and the media.

   Atkinson does not criticize the suicide figures on the basis of their inaccuracy, as he does not accept that there is an objectively real rate of suicide which can be discovered. The suicide rate is just a list of coroners' decisions.

   You could develop similar arguments applying your knowledge and understanding of health, church attendance, poverty and other official statistics.

(d) Using material from the *Items* and elsewhere, assess the usefulness of secondary data, other than official statistics, as sources of information. *(8 marks)*

Secondary data is information which has not been collected by the sociologists themselves but by others. It exists in either a quantitative or a qualitative form.

   Secondary sources used by sociologists include:
   ► **official statistics**;
   ► **organizational records**;
   ► **media output**;
   ► **diaries, autobiographies and other personal documents**; and
   ► **published sociological research**.
You should only refer to official statistics when assessing the usefulness of other forms of secondary data.

   This answer requires explicit evaluation. Your conclusions need not be even-handed but you must consider both strengths and weaknesses.
Your conclusions might argue the case for different kinds of secondary data complementing primary research.

(e) Assess the factors which affect whether researchers choose to examine 'hard data' or life-documents (*Item C*). *(7 marks)*

You can examine and assess the influence of:
► theoretical influences.
The debate between scientific/positivism and interpretive sociology can be applied here, perhaps referring to the use made by researchers into suicide of official statistics, casenotes and suicide notes.
► practical considerations.
You might consider time, money and the availability of data. For example, there may be no statistical data available from a particular time or place.

   There are possible influences on the sociologist's choice of data which could be applied to this question, such as:
► the topic being studied; and
► research ethics.

Question 2   Family

(a) What is the total percentage of households in Britain headed by a lone parent of either gender (*Item C*)? *(1 mark)*

20 per cent.

(b) *Item A* gives reasons suggested by functionalists and Marxists for 'male superiority' in the family. Give *two* criticisms of this functionalist view and *two* criticisms of this Marxist view. *(4 marks)*

One mark for each acceptable criticism up to a maximum of two for each perspective.
Functionalism
1 There is no general agreement on the ranking of skills and responsibility.
2 Women may hold 'important positions' in society.
Marxism
1 Biological fatherhood is not the only basis for inheritance by children.
2 Family relationships may not be determined by economic relationships.

(c) How might a feminist explain 'male superiority' in the family (*Item A*)? *(5 marks)*

There is no single feminist explanation of male superiority in the family. Some feminists may indeed challenge the persistence of male superiority.
   Marxist feminists emphasize the influence of the employment relationship and capitalism's requirement of a reserve army of labour.
   Some radical feminists offer a psychoanalytical explanation influenced by aspects of Freudian psychology.
   The ability and willingness of men to exercise violent control remains a theme of some feminist studies.
   Most feminist writers see an important role for patriarchal ideology in perpetuating male superiority in the family.

(d) Using examples, discuss the extent to which sociologists agree that childhood is a social construction (*Item B*). *(7 marks)*

You should present the evidence and arguments which support the view that childhood is a social construction and sufficient evaluation to provide a balanced answer. Explicit evaluation in a separate part of the answer is fine.
1 The biological/psychological view that childhood is a distinct natural phase of lifecycle ended by maturation. Some functionalist views on the family seem to implicitly accept this view.
2 Evidence that ideas about childhood vary from time to time and place to place.
3 Evidence for the social construction of childhood and perhaps the relative significance of gender from studies of childhood (Aires), the family, education and the media.
4 Arguments for a distinctive universal experience of childhood perhaps using functionalist, Marxist, new right and even feminist material on the family, gender and education.

(e) With reference to *Items C* and *D*, and other sources, assess sociological contributions to an understanding of lone-parent families. *(8 marks)*

Probably the most straightforward approach to this question is to assess a series of different theoretical perspectives on lone-parent families.
   Do not just list them and hope that this will provide sufficient evaluation. Your assessment should be explicit and not merely a juxtaposition of potentially critical approaches.

The obvious perspectives to consider are:

▶ **Functionalism**

Pessimistic functionalists equate the absence of a parent with family disorganization. Optimistic functionalists point out successful ways in which the absence of a parent can be 'compensated' for.

▶ **New right**

See lone-parent families as dysfunctional, likely to be welfare dependent and reproduce poverty and deviance. The Welfare State is blamed for encouraging single parenthood. This is mostly assertion and anecdote and less attention is paid to the death of a partner or the dysfunctions within two-parent families.

▶ **Feminists**

Are critical of families which are seen as both the cause and location of patriarchal domination. The harsh treatment of lone-parent families by the State is condemned and seen as a means of enforcing the dependence of women on the State and/or men.

This is not an exhaustive list. Neither do you have to consider all three perspectives.

Question 3   Education

(a) By how many percentage points do Afro–Caribbean women out-perform white women in gaining A-level qualifications or above (*Item C*)?   *(1 mark)*

6

(or 6 percentage points, *not 6%*. If you are not clear, ask your sociology or maths teacher)

(b) Name two programmes of compensatory education (*Item D*).   *(2 marks)*

Operation Headstart
Educational Priority Areas
Or: reasonable alternatives

(c) Assess the importance of pupils' subcultures in influencing educational attainment (*Items A* and *B*).   *(7 marks)*

You should explain the importance of pupils' subcultures and also demonstrate an awareness of other factors in educational attainment.
    Studies (e.g. Willis, Hargreaves, Fuller) should not just be described but applied to the issue of educational attainment.
    Your evaluation should be explicit, not just a list of different points of view.

(d) With reference to *Item C* and other information, evaluate sociological contributions to an understanding of the educational achievement of ethnic minorities in Britain.   *(8 marks)*

Item C should be used as instructed. It raises the issue of the interaction of gender and ethnicity in influencing achievement. It also goes on to look at the relationship between educational achievement and jobs.
    The other items suggest different sociological explanations which you may wish to apply to the question of ethnicity and educational attainment. These include:
▶ interactionist and subcultural theories (*Item A*)
▶ the influence of class relations on interaction in the school (*Item B*)
▶ compensatory education programmes and cultural deprivation (*Item D*)
You can use any other specific studies which explain the differential educational achievement of ethnic minorities. Your evaluation should be explicit and a conclusion offered. You may wish to refer to the problems of defining both educational achievement and indeed ethnicity. There is also the changing and contradictory nature of evidence which can be used to evaluate research.

(e) To what extent do sociologists agree with the idea that compensatory education programmes (*Item D*) have helped pupils from 'bad home-backgrounds' (*Item A*)? *(7 marks)*

You can explain how such programmes have provided help to certain targeted groups, generally identified by class and ethnicity.

Assessment of the success of the programmes may refer to specific research or make more general points about the problems for pupils lying in the school not the home, or the failure of education to compensate for more general social inequality. Halsey, among others, suggests that compensatory education was never really tried in Britain as so little money was attached to the programmes.

Question 4   Stratification

(a) According to *Item B*, what is the difference between the percentage of full-time university students from Social Class I and the percentage from Social Class V? *(1 mark)*

19%

(b) What do sociologists mean by the statement that increased mobility is the result of 'occupational change rather than increased opportunities for individual mobility' (*Item A*)? *(2 marks)*

The changes in the occupational structure mean there are more middle-class jobs. However, the chances of individuals from disadvantaged backgrounds achieving higher-class jobs in competition with those from more advantaged backgrounds has not improved significantly.

(c) In what ways do sociologists believe that levels of social mobility affect the importance of class identity (*Item C*)? *(4 marks)*

Item C offers some useful points which can be interpreted and applied to this question.

There are references to low social mobility, social closure and self-recruitment which maintain the homogeneity of the working and upper classes and reinforce class identity.

Conversely the references to increased social mobility into the service class might weaken identity.

You may wish to employ concepts such as class consciousness, false consciousness and/or refer to studies of industrial action, voting or other expressions of class conflict (or the lack of it).

(d) With reference to the *Items* and elsewhere, assess the argument that there is still a high level of self-recruitment in the British class structure. *(9 marks)*

Again the *Items* contain some useful points.
Item A discusses the continued self-recruitment of some ethnic minorities to lower social classes. This can be challenged by using empirical or theoretical evidence and arguments.
Item B encourages you to review the effect of higher education on social mobility.
Item C mentions the working, middle and upper classes and might encourage you to look at the effect of fragmentation of the class structure on self-recruitment.

(e) With reference to *Item A* and other sources, evaluate sociological explanations of the class position of ethnic minorities. *(9 marks)*

Remember that the question requires *explicit evaluation* not just the listing of alternative theories.

You can assess the strengths and weaknesses of these or other suitable explanations:

▶ **Marxist:** perhaps pointing out different Marxist views on the existence of a unified working class, or one with 'racialized fractions'.

▶ **Weberian:** examine the existence of an ethnically differentiated underclass. Perhaps challenge with empirical as well as theoretical arguments.

Of less importance you might look at:

▶ **functionalist theory**; and

▶ **new right:** views on an underclass.

Answers to timed practice paper 2

Question 1   Politics
Evaluate the claim made by some sociologists that there is a 'dominant ideology' in modern capitalist societies. *(25 marks)*

You can enhance your answer to this question by reference to one or more of the other topic areas you have studied. The concept of ideology is very useful in topics such as the family, education, media and religion.

Most candidates who attempt this question will at least be able to outline a generalized Marxist perspective which identifies a 'dominant ideology' in capitalist societies.

Better answers will be able to distinguish the variations between different Marxist approaches, as well as alternatives to the Marxist views.

Outline answer

1 Discuss a variety of Marxist and neo-Marxist views.
Useful concepts include:

▶ superstructure;

▶ false consciousness;

▶ hegemony; and

▶ ISAs and RSAs.

You can mention the internal Marxist debate between instrumentalists and structuralists.

2 Critical views which challenge the existence of a dominant ideology include:

▶ **Marxists** who see the importance of ideological control diminishing with control being exercised through the employment relationship.

▶ **Pluralists** who see a number of competing ideologies and political ideas and institutions. The media are generally seen in a positive light.

▶ **Functionalists** who may very well identify certain dominant ideas but do not see these as imposed by a ruling class and only representing sectional interests. Instead they see consensual values which reinforce social solidarity. You might refer here to the family and education.

Question 2   Religion
'Durkheim's view that religion reinforces the collective conscience of society is more appropriate to an understanding of small, non-literate societies, than it is to large, modern and diversified societies.' Critically examine this argument. *(25 marks)*

Candidates may have some difficulty applying their prepared general knowledge of the major theories to this apparently specific question.

A generalized account of functionalist theory with marginal reference to the issues raised in the question will gain marks but miss the opportunity to do well.

As always with questions on the role of religion, the application of contemporary examples will be rewarded.

Outline answer

An outline of Durkheim's functionalist perspective on religion focusing on the way religion reinforces the collective conscience of society. Explain the existence of central values which integrate society.

Criticism can take various forms:

1 Agree with the proposition in the question that the function of religion may be the integration of simple societies but is less applicable, or not applicable at all, to complex modern societies. You could discuss:
- the secularization of modern society;
- the absence of a single undisputed faith in modern society;
- sectarianism and NRMs; and
- cultural/ethnic diversity.

2 Modern functionalist views which do see religion as contributing to social solidarity, for example, Parsons, Herberg.

3 The Marxist rejection of functionalism and all consensus theories. The Marxist perspective on the function of religion in society which emphasizes false consciousness rather than the collective conscience.

Question 3   Poverty

Assess the sociological evidence for and against the argument that the Welfare State both creates and perpetuates a culture of dependency. *(25 marks)*

A good answer to this question will provide more than a general account of studies of poverty and the Welfare State.

The sociological evidence and arguments should be focused on the relationship between the Welfare State and a possible culture of dependency.

Your evidence may be presented within a theoretical framework similar to that suggested in Chapter 5 on poverty.

Good answers may demonstrate the links between:
- sociological theory;
- social policy; and
- some of the current moral and ideological debates about a dependency culture.

There is no single right answer. You could concentrate on the culture of poverty but it is also legitimate to discuss related issues such as:
- unemployment;
- single-parent families; and
- health.

You are not required to cover these or other less central concerns and they must be related to the set question.

Outline answer

You should assess the strengths and weaknesses of some of the following arguments:
- The new right

Has condemned the Welfare State for both creating and perpetuating a culture of dependency.

Universal benefits have been particularly criticized.

Some recipients, such as single mothers and young men, have been singled out for criticism.

▶ The culture of poverty
   Some views identify a culture of poverty and see the poor as a distinct group.
   Dependency may be part of this culture.
   They rarely, however, see the Welfare State as a significant factor in either the
   creation or perpetuation of this culture – or, indeed, poverty itself.
▶ Social Democrats
   See the causes of poverty lying in the structure of society.
   The Welfare State does not create a culture of dependency but it may help to
   perpetuate it.
   Inadequate means-tested benefits create a poverty trap.
▶ Marxists
   Reject the notion of a culture of dependency and see the causes of poverty
   lying in the inevitable inequalities of capitalist society.
   The Welfare State is viewed critically.
▶ Feminists
   Some feminists see the Welfare State as contributing to the enforced
   dependence of women on men. The patriarchal ideology of the family is
   important to this process.

Question 4   Deviance

'The usefulness of crime statistics in sociological research depends on the
theoretical approach adopted by the sociologist.' Critically explain this view.
(25 marks)

> You should prepare a critical discussion of the usefulness of secondary data
> and in particular official statistics for questions on theory and methods as
> well as specific topics.
>   The debate over Durkheim's study of suicide is often used by books and
> teachers to discuss both the theoretical and methodological issues involved.
>   This question, however, requires a focus on crime statistics rather than
> suicide statistics and you must apply your arguments appropriately.
>   A response that only points out the limited uses of crime statistics,
> without reference to theoretical issues, will not score a high mark and
> misses the opportunity to use ideas about positivism and critics that nearly
> all students will have considered during their studies.

Outline answer

1 Positivists follow the model of Durkheim's 'suicide' and use crime statistics to
   formulate and test hypotheses about the causes of crime and the characteristics
   of offenders and victims.
2 Positivists are not uncritical of the use of crime statistics based on crimes
   known to the police and may be concerned with their *reliability, representativeness*
   and *completeness*.
3 These problems have been identified and to some extent addressed by the use
   of:
   ▶ victim studies;
   ▶ self-report studies; and
   ▶ other sources of data, such as child line and rape crisis centres.
4 Intepretive sociologists have questioned the *validity* of crime statistics. They see
   them as socially constructed by the agencies who collect and interpret them.
       Rather than *use* crime statistics to study crime, sociologists such as
   J.M. Atkinson argue that the statistics are a topic worth studying in their own
   right. The statistics are seen as neither accurate nor inaccurate as a record of
   crime. Instead, they reveal the commonsense assumptions of the police, the
   judicial system, the media and the public in general.
5 You may refer to the systematic bias in the statistics claimed by Marxists, new
   criminologists and feminists.

LONGMAN
EXAM
PRACTICE
KITS

REVISION PLANNER

Getting Started — *Begin on week 12*

Use a calendar to put dates onto your planner and write in the dates of your exams. Fill in your targets for each day. Be realistic when setting the targets, and try your best to stick to them. If you miss a revision period, remember to re-schedule it for another time.

Get Familiar — *Weeks 12 and 11*

Identify the topics on your syllabuses. Get to know the format of the papers – time, number of questions, types of questions. Start reading through your class notes, coursework, etc.

Get Serious — *Week 10*

Complete reading through your notes – you should now have an overview of the whole syllabus. Choose 12 topics to study in greater depth for each subject. Allocate two topic areas for each subject for each of the next 6 weeks

No. of weeks before the exams	Date: Week commencing	MONDAY	TUESDAY
12			
11			
10			

WEDNESDAY	THURSDAY	FRIDAY	SATURDAY	SUNDAY

LONGMAN

No. of weeks before the exams	Date: Week commencing	MONDAY	TUESDAY
9			
8			
7			
6			
5			
4			
3			
2			
1			

LONGMAN EXAM PRACTICE KITS:
Titles Available –

GCSE
Biology
Business Studies
Geography
Mathematics
Physics
Science

A-LEVEL
Biology
Business Studies
Chemistry
Mathematics
Psychology
Sociology

There are lots of ways to revise. It is important to find what works best for you. Here are some suggestions:

• try testing with a friend: testing each other can be fun!
• label or highlight sections of text and make a checklist of these items.
• learn to write summaries – these will be useful for revision later.
• try reading out loud to yourself.
• don't overdo it – the most effective continuous revision session is probably between forty and sixty minutes long.
• practise answering past exam papers and test yourself using the same amount of time as you will have on the actual day – this will help to make the exam itself less daunting.
• pace yourself, taking it step by step.

WEDNESDAY	THURSDAY	FRIDAY	SATURDAY	SUNDAY

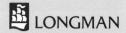